You Are Already A

Wife...

Long Before
The First Date!

The Character Building Guide for Women
Called by God to Wifedom

by Latoyia K. Bailey, PhD
Foreword by Apostle Thomas Wesley Weeks, Sr.

Calla Lily Publishing
Where We Read for Evidence

You Are Already a Wife...Long Before The First Date!
Published by Calla Lily Publishing
P.O. Box 1061
Brookhaven, PA 19015
Email: callalilypublishing@gmail.com

© 2010 by Latoyia K. Bailey, PhD
Cover design and layout by Lindsay M. Deisher

All the stories mentioned in the book are true, but many of the names of those involved have been expunged to protect the privacy of these individuals.

Unless otherwise indicated, all Scripture quotations marked (NIV) are taken from the HOLY BIBLE, NEW INTERNATIONAL VERSION. Copyright c 1973, 1978, 1984 International Bible Society. Used by permission of Zondervan Bible Publishers. All rights reserved. Scripture quotations marked (NKJV) are taken from the New King James Version. Copyright © 1979, 1980, 1982 by Thomas Nelson, Inc. Used by permission. All rights reserved. Scripture quotations marked (KJV) are taken from the King James Version of the Holy Bible.

Bailey, Latoyia K., 1973 –
You are already a wife... long before the first date! / Latoyia K. Bailey.

Includes bibliographical references.
ISBN-13: 978-0-615-39782-5
1. Christian Living   2. Love and Marriage   3. Women – Single   I. Title.
Library of Congress Control Number: 2010915696

Printed in the United States of America

"*You* don't wait until you have the title in order to walk in your authority. A title only confirms it!"

- Apostle Thomas Wesley Weeks, Sr.

This book is dedicated to my mother, Mrs. Rose Anne Kline for her constant and effectual, fervent prayers in which the Lord availeth much. It is my mother's unconditional love that continues to resonate as the epitome of wifedom in a God-given ministry.

And it is also written in remembrance of Mrs. Sandra L. Brooks who, before entering wifedom, always embodied the esthetic, character, wisdom, and virtue of her womanhood. With grace, she showed many women that the voids felt in singleness were those linked to the lies created in the battlefield of one's own mind.

Contents

Foreword by Apostle Thomas Wesley Weeks, Sr.   v

Introduction   1

Part One
The Process of the Promise: Purging, Purity, & Peace

Chapter One   6
Weeping May Endure for a Night

Chapter Two   11
Yes, It Is Possible! *(Your Help May be in Developing
Someone Else's Boaz)*

Chapter Three   19
He Knows What's Best for You

Chapter Four   23
What Has God Promised You?

Part Two
Persevere by Following the Pilot's Plan
Through Prayer, Patience, & Poise

Chapter Five   28
You Cannot Appoint Your Own Seat

Chapter Six   32
Learn to Look Beyond the Obvious

Chapter Seven   40
Submissive Doesn't Mean Passive

Chapter Eight   51
Know Your Worth

$\mathcal{P}$art Three
Proceed with Power and Praise –
Posture Yourself for This Wifedom Position

Chapter Nine   60
Preach to Your Promise but Minister to that Man

Chapter Ten
If It's Early, It Could Die   70
From Bitter Pain Comes the Birthing of Instruction   72

Chapter Eleven
Have a Deep Resolve – Firm Determination   77
The Triad Experience   84

Chapter Twelve
Be Happy, Be Free, and Be Filled!   87
(Allow God to Get the Glory Out of Your Story)
Look to the Hills   93
SEX B4 Marriage: The Real BFF (**B**roken   96
Future **F**antasies)
Stand Still + Calm Down = Watch God   101

Acknowledgments

With special thanks:

To Bishop Thomas Wesley Weeks, Sr. and my New Destiny Fellowship Church family for showing me the value in birthing a ministry out of my misery. The many years of reaching, teaching, and fellowship have shown me that true wisdom lies in earnest listening rather than hasty responses.

To Colton Jones because this book would still just be a journal full of private notes, tear-stained prayers, and closet confessions if it were not for his promptings. He was the one who kept asking me, "What's next?" when I thought the hard work was already done and was ready to celebrate a little too early. Thank you for encouraging me to make goals and see them through until the end.

To my editor, Mrs. Judy Harper, for your honesty, creativity, and open-mindedness, which encouraged me to remain a broken vessel for the Lord.

To my parents, Lawrence and Rose Anne Kline, for paving the way and being God-given examples of how a good marriage works.

To my sister, Olivia K. Bailey, and my dad, Oliver K. Eason, for the monetary support which paved the way for countless fundraisers. Olivia, I would never be able to stay in contact with "the outside world" if it were not for you.

To my grandmothers-in-the-spirit, June Broadus and Rose Davis, who consistently met me at the Threshing Floor at the most crucial times during my walk through this book project. Your encouragement, prayer support, and message of 'good news' kept me stable from glory to glory.

To my goddaughter Callie M. Rozier, whose warm and endearing smile lights my way. Thank you for giving the best hugs and kisses – the ones that make me feel as though I can conquer anything.

To Hannah Tran for your insightful ideas and bursts of energy. Thank you for making "work" just a little easier to handle and helping me to meet those deadlines.

To my sister-circle of friends, family, and supporters who listened, prayed, and continue to be my personal cheerleaders: Tyricka M. Rozier, Kiana L. Thompson, Luana McMurray-Hodges, Stephanie N. James Wilson, Norma Lee, Latanya Bonnette, Dr. Marcia Taylor, Dr. Iya Adjua, Michelle Butler, Adrienne Eason, Keesha Ransom, Linda Haskins, Tami Tillman, Sharon Thomas, Melody Baysmore, and Dr. Adrienne Chew.

To Dawn and Greg Morris, the "dynamic duo" for being such motivating inspirations! When I grow up, I want to be like you! You have personally shown me there is no 'I' in team.

Foreword

A short while ago, I read an article about a young man who hit the lottery for tens of millions of dollars. He had just been found buried in a friend's backyard after being missing for a few months. This man had just confessed to a close family member that he wished he were broke again. Unfortunately, he got what he wanted but was unprepared for what came with it. There are character traits one needs in life to handle riches. Likewise there are character traits you need in your life for a successful marriage that may not seem necessary when single.

In this book, Dr. Bailey makes the urgent point that before getting what we want, we had better ensure we have the character to support the desire. Our nation is facing a major dilemma with marriages. The divorce rate is over 50% and only one parent is leading a majority of families. The problem and solution does not just lie on the doorsteps of the male. Both male and female bear responsibility for this tragic statistic. It is your responsibility to prepare for all that you desire and are praying to acquire.

This book is a must-read for every woman who has contemplated marriage, yet carries in her memory the wounds of past relationships; it explains and cancels pain and replaces that with gratitude as it teaches you how to grow in your process of becoming a wife.

Dr. Bailey informs us that the waiting we have been complaining about might be a major blessing in disguise. Not only should the time be used to grow, mature, and heal, it should also be used to prepare for the right one. The book not only gives recognition to the fact that some near-perfect men were never meant to be your husband, it explains the reasons you should have been happy to let them pass. To help you with this challenge, she shares an eternal truth; *do not prize the gift more than the giver*.

Among the many truths, you will learn the power and blessing of anticipatory prayer. We are not perfect; neither are our mates. Prayer helps us overcome the shortcomings in the relationship and gives room for change to take place. Prayer does change things!

Because you do not have a minute to lose or waste, start reading and put what you learn to work. It will not take long before you start thanking God for all of the lessons Dr. Bailey learned on your behalf. Her willingness to be transparent is to your benefit so that you can be everything God has called you to be.

-Apostle Thomas Wesley Weeks, Sr.
Founder, New Destiny Fellowship

Introduction

*F*or a very long time, I have been adding to the chapters of my future as a wife – looking at my *wifedom* experience through a single woman's eyes. Even before I know who my husband will be, God has given me the unction to author this book uncovering truths about the role of becoming a wife. None other than God would let me know my testimony before the completion of my test! He is awesome!

And you, you are not reading this by accident. After you read this book, you too will come to understand your role as a wife – long before your future husband's first phone call or date. You are going to come to realize that of the many functions and roles you will play, one of them will be to pray for your future husband and keep him covered. This means that in difficult times, instead of complaining to your sister-friends and your family, you will need to go to his Head, Jesus Christ, and pray for him.

> *Now I want you to realize that the head of*
> *every man is Christ, and the head of the woman is*
> *man, and the head of Christ is God.*
> *1 Corinthians 11:3 NIV*

How much more difficult praying is when you have no name, face, or image of your husband. Each day when you rise, as you pray for yourself, you ought to pray for him as well. Keep him covered, protected, and guided. That is just *one* of your duties as a wife. Can everyone do this? Not easily, but it's definitely necessary. And believe it or not, your husband may not be the only man the Lord has given you an intercessory charge over. As you sow into the lives of other men like your brothers, father, friends, cousins, and even ex-boyfriends, you also sow into the life of your husband and any son you may have. It's called *karma*. Whether you believe it or not, the positive energy that you put out into the universe does find its way back to you. The same is true about negative energy as well. Wifedom starts with ministering into the lives of other men who may never be *your* husband.

When God tells you that wifedom is in your future, your role begins from the moment of His word, not the moment you lay eyes on your engagement ring. When God told me about my wifedom, I hadn't even started getting calls from men! Nevertheless, He told me to wake early in the morning, anoint my head, mouth, feet, ears, eyes, and hands to pray – pray in the spirit for my husband and for my future. Sound crazy? Maybe, but remember, His ways are not our ways. You have to hear His words in your spirit.

> *As for God, his way is perfect; the word of*
> *the Lord is flawless. He is a shield for all those*
> *who take refuge in him.*
> *2 Samuel 22:31 NIV*

and

> *'For my thoughts are not your thoughts, neither*
> *are your ways my ways,' declares the Lord.*
> *Isaiah 55:8 NIV*

As God is working in your life to perfect you in the kingdom of wives for what your husband needs, you are anointed to practice the weight of God's principle, the principle of binding and loosing. You will bind on earth (that which you see and will see) so that it is also bound in heaven (that which you cannot see), and whatever you loose on earth will be loosed in heaven (Matthew 16:19 NIV). Your task is to arrest spirits on behalf of your future husband before they can attack him, you, or your future family. Remember, you were created to be a helpmate for him. *Now* is the time to become that, so that he can actually make it safely to you.

> *The Lord God said, "It is not good for the*
> *man to be alone. I will make a helper suitable for*
> *him."*
> *Genesis 2:18 NIV*

The covenant and union of marriage is about your cleaving to become one. Therefore, as you pray for yourself, you must *also* pray for him. As you receive blessings, so does he and vice versa. We have to stop expecting God to do *all* of the work. There are things that we must accomplish before God will do His part – that which we cannot do. And remember, faith without works is dead.

> *As the body without the spirit is dead, so faith*
> *without deeds is dead.*
> *James 2:26 NIV*

It is your husband's nakedness, his enemies (namely fears, weaknesses, and insecurities) that you are supposed to cover from the world.

For this reason a man will leave his father and
mother and be unified. To his wife, and they will
become one flesh. The man and his wife were
both naked, they felt no shame.
Genesis 2:24-25 NIV

Did you ever try to give up on a dream or goal that God put deep down in your heart – so deep that you felt it was part of your soul? And did you come to a point where you knew the Holy Spirit living on the inside of you was not going to allow you to let it go – no matter how much you tried? That should tell you something. Usually, we want to give up when we are so busy looking at the natural – what everyone else has and what we don't see in our own lives. That can kill the dream God put on the inside of you. Don't let it. It's Satan's plan for you to denounce the promise and turn away from it. Remember that Satan only knows the lie – but you've been told the truth. Throughout the process of reading, you will begin to uncover many hidden issues about yourself – issues you never knew existed. Right now, make a promise to yourself that you will do the work necessary to go through the process of change and transformation that it will take to reach the promises of God.

Part One

The Process of the Promise:
Purging, Purity, and Peace

*God already made the
Promise, now steady yourself
through the Process.*

Chapter 1

Weeping May Endure for a Night....

The hardest thing I ever had to admit to myself was that I wasn't really ready for marriage. Although it came as a pure shock to me, what made it especially difficult was, I felt that since I was getting older, marriage had to be in the very near future. Desperate, and with every waking day, I wanted it more and more! However, deep down inside, I knew that I really wasn't ready – not the kind of ready God had in mind. Gradually, I realized that there were lessons God had prepared for me, character building that would take place, people who I was appointed and assigned to help, and goals I had to accomplish before being partnered as a wife. I asked myself, how could I get my personal timetable to fit in with God's timing? Finally I had to realize and accept that there were too many things God had set in motion that had to take place *before* reaching my appointed time with my future husband.

Revelation can be a beautiful thing, but I cannot explain to you in mere words the feeling of anguish and sadness that selfishly came over me. How was I yet mature enough to handle being the kind of wife God was preparing me to be, when all I could think about were my needs, my wants, and my age – what about *my* predetermined way out?

When you start to attend at least three weddings a year between your girlfriends and your associates, you begin to wonder, "What's wrong with me?" I had to remember that just because those women had reached their appointed time with their husbands that did not have any bearing on God's vision for my life. And neither will your appointed time come any sooner if you too, neglect or delay the opportunities and goals God has for you. You cannot measure yourself by another's timetable and determine that theirs is where God wants you to operate.

You already believe He is sovereign: there is no turning back. Since He is sovereign, are you ready to believe that He has a unique plan specifically designed to prepare you for the marriage He has for you? Are you ready to act on your marriage preparedness plan in *every* area of your life?

God is going to lovingly purge us of everything that would ultimately ruin the union that we so desire: I repeat, He purges or we ruin. Fighting His kingdom principles will only delay us from keeping our so-desired appointment. Remember, although the Lord is a gentleman, He will not make us adhere to what He has set up. Because of His love for us, He will continually prompt us to move toward His promises.

Why do you want a husband? Is it because you need a father for your children? You want someone to help you pay the bills? You finally want to be able to have sex without sinning or to alleviate the feeling of condemnation? Or do you want a husband because *you* need a helpmate or because you feel the need to *be* one? Be honest with yourself about why you really want a husband since God knows the truth anyway. Don't feed into the desire out of a carnal or fleshly need. Refer to Genesis 2. Why was Eve created for Adam? God created her out of Adam's rib, out of *his* need for a helpmate, not the other way around. Your husband's main purpose is not just to protect you and pay your bills. His purpose in your life is so much more than that.

The purpose of this book is to take your yielded heart to God to get an understanding of the hard places you may have to tread through before you are married. You may have to weep, endure extended periods of alone time and spend time nurturing a man who will never be *your* husband. You may have to fend off many questions and those *why you aren't married yet* looks from others. Fear and anxiety may set in and lead to a tendency to try to get out of your designed assignments before they are completed. If you do that, you end up aborting God's promise for your life. *Singlehood is* an assignment. To be effective in your role as a wife, each one of you has to spend some time alone. Ester did and so did Rachel. The time that you spend alone actually is time well spent with the Lord. If you let Him, God will use the opportunity to minister to you and to fellowship with you.

On the eve of one particular New Year, I was drawn to watch Bishop T.D. Jakes. He asked his congregation an intriguing question, "Why is the night so long – lasting days, weeks, or even months at times?" I had spent a night of crying over God's promise of marriage. Yes, actually crying over a *promise*. The tears were for the promise that had not found its way to me by the end of yet another year. Time and patience always seem to get the better of me and on this night, not forty-five seconds into the message, I started to weep because I knew, in that moment, that I was exactly where God wanted me. Bishop Jakes' message was "God of the Night Before," and there I was in the "night before" moment in my life - that period of time when I want to give up because I feel stupid or afraid of what others might think. I had developed into my own worst critic. It was in that moment I realized that I needed to stay peaceful and on the high road. God's perfect timing would answer me, and the worst of critics, but I had to *faint not*. I had to take the steps of faith that God had placed on the inside of me. Singlehood is a preparation time. We must spend it well for the man we are to marry may be prepared and ready.

Some women believe that there are no men who really want to get married. That is a lie straight from hell. There *are* men who do desire life mates. It is you who must be prepared. First, allow God to show you your husband's needs before He can show you who he is. They too, have a process to complete and unfortunately, many are still ill-equipped and do not know what their real purpose in life is. They too, must go through the same process as Adam – a period of naming as he first did with the animals. Of course, I'm not calling women animals; however, I am making the point that as the sons of Adam, men also need the opportunity to understand the reason and the purpose of every one in which they come into contact. Their alone time with God and their purpose for being without us as well as their wives may be for many reasons.

Viewing things in the natural, it simply looks like men have too many women to choose from. But in the spiritual, women have always been an important part of a much bigger plan – a God-ordained plan; it's not the enemy's doing as some women may actually believe. It's natural for a man to see just what is out there so that they can recognize a wife when the Lord places her in front of him. It's quite difficult for men to tell who we are in their lives; God must tell them. Many women are indirectly available to men who watch them interact with others, read their character, test their strength, and assess the mirror of their virtue. Sad thing is, too many of those men may not even know that's what they are doing! Sometimes, God can truly reveal a woman's purpose in a man's life, but that man may not understand it for years to come.

Some women want a particular man so badly that they begin to develop and undertake desperate schemes just to get him. Most of us know a woman or two who may have said that "desperate times call for desperate measures". As a consequence, for far too many singles, the institution of dating has turned into premarital mating, which further complicates God's institution of marriage. Even if you believe that God has spoken to *you* about whom your husband is, that does not grant you permission to take action with your own hands. That is *not* your place. That right belongs to the Lord. Involving yourself in God's business and being out of His timing may delay your progress and cause your future husband to resent you if you tell him what you *think* you know. The lesson is between that man and God. Stay in God's timing – stay in your place. Weeping may endure for a night, but joy will come in the morning.

Chapter 2

Yes, It Is Possible! *Your Help May be in Developing Someone Else's Future Boaz*

Conversations with other women have made me conclude that at times it does become necessary to remove oneself from the life of what seems like a good man because God has directed it. An explanation is, alone time or times of isolation are set aside by God to build character, to foster more growth in Christ or to position either person for a place of authority or completion in Him. Without this alone process, we cannot take our rightful position next to another as a partner, confidant, lover, or supporter. Women are nurturers by nature and some tend to believe that failed relationships only need time for healing. However, the adage about God closing doors and opening windows is nothing to play with. The struggle to pry open doors that God has already closed can only lead to frustration, a loss of precious time, and a lack of trust in God's will and direction for your own life.

Many women are blessed to have healthy, platonic friendships with those of the opposite sex. Usually, their friendships are a blessing to both the man and woman involved. When a woman is blessed with the opportunity to touch the life of a *Boaz* type of man, she is placed there to make distinct differences and affect positive changes in his life.

Many women have backwards thinking. When you watch the man you have grown to love in the Lord develop into the very Boaz you had envisioned for yourself, it will be difficult to realize, accept and admit that maybe he isn't *your* Boaz. Too many women have become distraught enough that they walk out of God's purpose and remove themselves from friendships with good men because revelation has set in: those men were never called to be their husbands. It will take a great letting go mentality to be grateful and actually thankful to God that He has entrusted you with another woman's Boaz to enrich your personal circle. The most important aspect of it all is your attitude about the situation. Do you complain because the man before you isn't necessarily the *one* for you? Or do you murmur while standing enviously outside his other relationship and pose judgment? Instead of affecting change and walking into purpose, backwards thinking would allow you to reshape or alter the men in an ungodly manner; instead, use your positive influence by operating in the authority of your God-given position.

Keep your eyes fixated on the main thing – the true purpose for the relationship or friendship. The Lord of your life, the Lover of your soul is *always* the main thing. That man's salvation and renewed spirit is also a main thing, not any control that you have over him or any manipulation over the situation. This special time and special assignment should be kept in the right perspective. If you truly believe that "God will supply all your needs according to His riches in glory," then you have to know that every single thing will work out for your good and in your best interest (Philippians 4:19 KJV). Since God has favored and entrusted you with this type of relationship, one of your goals from this day forward should be to keep the right attitude about the situation.

Just as detrimental to the heart is the ending of another type of relationship, especially when it takes a different turn and *God* says it's over. You have no clue why it is, but – guess what, it's over! Continuing to befriend or even help those He has already told you to leave alone is no different from people who chose to openly defy God's will. I am reminded of the scripture that warns, "Do not give what is holy to the dogs; nor cast your pearls before swine, lest they trample them under their feet and turn and tear you in pieces" (Matthew 7:6 NKJV). Although this is not a rule, its issuance by God is a chance for you to show your love, trust, and commitment toward the walk He's planned for your life; it is a matter of heart safety and emotional stability. It's hard to admit, but keeping people in your life that God has instructed you to leave alone is an overall act of defiance, which could lead directly to sin. Since God is sovereign, sometimes we cannot understand why it was alright to befriend and talk to a person last month but feel an annoyance in one's spirit when trying to strike up a mere conversation the next month. Don't even try to figure it out. Just trust and adhere to His direction, because going against God's will can and usually does affect a blessing somewhere down the line.

Unlike the women who walked away after developing a Boaz for another, there are those relationships that end when a friend or significant other leaves your life. In these cases, your lack of clarity may lead to ill-feelings. Those ill-feelings can lead to a sense of abandonment, loss of direction, unrest and upsets that have to be dealt with in the aftermath. This is when the guessing game begins. Why is it that when unwanted change happens abruptly and failed expectations appear suddenly, we feel the need to press replay on the events we believe caused the disappointment in the first place? Could it be our compulsive need to control the situation? Or is it our fear that unpremeditated break-ups and blanketed miscommunication will only spiral into further confusion? I'm a firm believer that everything comes full circle. There will come a time when you realize it's more of a blessing than a curse when someone leaves your life. As difficult as it may sound, those who leave our lives do so because we probably weren't strong enough to leave theirs. We don't always have to have the answers to everything in order to reach the level of peace and acceptance that God wants for us to press onward, for as Proverbs 3:5-6 NIV reads, "Trust in the Lord with all your heart and lean not on your own understanding; in all your ways acknowledge him, and he will make your paths straight."

The attitude of gratitude comes when you learn to develop what we will call the *gift of goodbye* – the ability to let go of those who can no longer bless your life. Many times, people come into our lives to fulfill a need or a purpose in their own lives that is ordained by God. Sometimes, to much dismay, we are left perplexed when God allows or even initiates their removal from the relationship. This is especially daunting when it transpires without any warning as it did for Philip and an Ethiopian eunuch who were traveling together, as described in Acts 8:38b-39 NIV:

> *Then both Philip and the eunuch went down into*
> *the water and Philip baptized him. When they*
> *came up out of the water, the Spirit of the Lord*
> *suddenly took Philip away, and the eunuch did*
> *not see him again, but went on his way rejoicing.*

This scripture should bring new hope. The spirit of the Lord ordained it, and the eunuch was not disappointed or even moved by his loss because his focus and his newfound drive was centered around the gift of the spirit. His focus was not on Philip himself, but on the gift deposited – his newly found connection to the Lord. The traveler knows that his life will never be the same because the Spirit of the Lord, through Philip, had touched him. Philip was a vehicle destined to fulfill a need for *that* time. Perhaps it's time for you to ask the Lord for the gift of goodbye.

When a man would leave my life or I felt the need to leave his, I felt distraught – like something was wrong with me or like I was making the wrong decision. Finally, God spoke to me and said there was nothing wrong with me except my inability to let go of that, which no longer had a place of blessing in my life. Whenever you've come to a crossroad in your life where you have to make an important decision that ultimately affects your relationship with others, that is the time to pay attention and watch for the signs. God always provides them – big and small. Signs come through the agitated feelings deep down in your spirit, messages in movies, the voice of a child, and even through gifts of the spirit such as dreams and visions.

Signs and signals are the Lord's constant reminder to you that not only is He aware of what is happening, but that He is also in control of it all. Nothing that you go through is a surprise to God. If you have never noticed the signs in your life, ask God for the ability to recognize them. In the book of Isaiah, Ahaz, the king of Judah was instructed by God Himself to ask for a sign that the kings of Aram and Ephraim would not invade Judah. But before Ahaz was instructed to ask for a sign, he was told to ". . . be careful, keep calm and don't be afraid. Do not lose heart because of these two smoldering stubs of firewood . . ." (Isaiah 7:4a NIV). It was important for God to send

Isaiah as a messenger to Ahaz beforehand so that Ahaz' faith would be strengthened. It doesn't matter how many signs of confirmation the Lord provides for you if you fail to stand firm in your faith. The fruits of the spirit are truly an outward manifestation of one's faith. In the end, in order to develop the gift of goodbye, you have to develop your faith and relationship with the Lord.

Quit trying to figure everything out and keep your eyes focused on the future, not the present. Joel Osteen says, "Get out of the safe zone and get into the faith zone." Although the "safe zone" may resemble a resting place, it may, however, become a dry brook – a place of stagnant discontent when one refuses to trust God and move into a level of change where a higher place of responsibility is required.

> **"Get out of the safe zone and get into the faith zone."**
> (Joel Osteen)

The safe zone was never meant to become a permanent place of refuge and hiding. That really is almost comical because there really is no such thing as hiding from God. However, there is such a thing as hiding from the truth – being afraid of one's new level of authority, role or responsibility.

While in the safe zone, have you turned away from something God has instructed you to do? Were you told to pray for a difficult person or to let go of a long time friend? Or maybe the Lord has instructed you to turn down a promotion at work or even move to another state. What area of your faith is the Lord now dealing with? Why would you continue to linger in the safe zone?

Enter into the faith zone. Don't be afraid to take a risk, that which God has already told you to take. You know that He is sovereign; therefore, every single thing that happens is for your overall benefit and will turn out for your good. It's been said that *it's hard to see the whole picture when you're inside the frame* and, *never automatically assume that God's delays are God's denials.* The faith zone is an area of process through preparation while lying prostrate before the Lord. It doesn't have to be a scary place. Quite the contrary, the faith zone is not a place filled with dangerous mines where one ought to be afraid of stepping out. It is a field of dreams where God's grace allows one to move freely while embracing His rod and staff, which are there to comfort and guide you. It is a place of newness, growth and miraculous change. Think about this – if you are having a difficult time walking by faith in the Lord, then how will you walk by faith *with your husband* in the Lord? No matter how strong in the Lord your future husband is becoming, you too will have to develop your very own faith zone experiences with the Lord your God. But fear not and welcome it. Since change is inevitable, walking in it with the Lord can be a glorious decision.

Consider it a blessing that you don't have to solve every problem or figure out every detail of your life on your own. As children of the Most High God, we get to leave that up to Him. As a matter of fact, we can get into works of the flesh when we try to figure out every minute detail of situations that are clearly beyond our limited understanding. In Deuteronomy 29:29a (NIV) the Word declares, "The secret things belong to the Lord our God." It's within God's privy to know everything. Perhaps He may reveal why some relationships or friendships had to end or why some people were never meant to stay with us, but He doesn't have to. Proverbs 25:2a (KJV) warns, "It is the glory of God to conceal" whatsoever He chooses. To have faith in Him means we don't have to have a full understanding of everything that happens in order to have peace with the outcome. Trusting in Him

> **"Worry is not a weakness – it's a wickedness. Worry is like telling God you don't trust Him."**
>
> (Bill Purvis)

means believing that whatever happens in the end, it definitely will work out for our own good. Remember, "Now we see but a poor reflection as in a mirror; then we shall see face to face. Now I know in part; then I shall know fully, even as I am fully known" (I Corinthians 13:12b NIV).

Because God loves us, He will give us clarity and a more complete understanding in due season – when we are mature enough to handle the *image* or new reflection set before us. Instead of carrying constant sorrow that often grows into bitterness and resentment, give it to the Lord. Become a gardener and plant the seedling that the devil *thinks* he has stolen from you. Trust God, be of good courage, and know that His timing is absolutely perfect in your life. Don't waste any more time – not one more day.

Chapter 3

He knows what's best for you

I can remember sitting on the edge of my bed crying because I wanted God to remove that cup from me – the cup of the responsibility of knowing that marriage would come one day, but not the day I had planned in my head. It actually became painful for me when I realized that although I wanted to be married, I was not ready for it despite all my longings. Before I admitted the truth to myself about my unpreparedness, God was already doing something new, something much needed within me. He was preparing me in a way much differently from what I was previously going through. The Teacher knows when to alter the lesson so that the student can still

> "God does not transfer without transforming. He delights in moving things from heaven to earth."
>
> (Apostle Thomas Wesley Weeks, Sr.)

learn from it – still pass the test and make a successful mark toward kingdom living. I thank Him for that. The tear-stained pillows and midnight talks with Jesus were all a part of the transitional lessons which are changing me into what He needs me to be, for He knows that it will ultimately lead me to become a much better person in the future. It's as simple as that. The Lord makes investments and deposits into our lives on a daily basis through His Word and through the manifestations of having a serious, loving, one-on-one relationship with Him. The bottom line is that it is *always* in your best interest to do what the Holy Spirit pours into your heart to do, no matter how you *feel* about it.

Some of you are probably wondering why I would share these truisms about my secret thoughts on marriage. For too long, people have feared singleness and have secretly thought of it as a punishment like the plague or an affliction. But that is as far from the truth as the east is from the west. Paul's explanation sums up your relationship with the Lord in 1 Corinthians 7:34b (NIV) with these words: "An unmarried woman or virgin is concerned about the Lord's affairs: Her aim is to be devoted to the Lord in both body and spirit." I used to have backwards thinking about marriage and a husband. And I also remember when God gently reminded me that He was my soul provider – my Jehovah Jirah.

It was the year I needed a new heater. In the dead of winter, it kept breaking down. I would wake up in the morning to a cold house and no hot water to bathe. Instead of getting ready for work, I found myself scared, frustrated, and feeling alone. The heating unit was old, and I needed about $5,000 to get a new one. I thought that I could rely on a man that I was dating at the time. I thought that he would offer to lend me some of the money that I needed for the replacement. Well, the only thing he offered was a spare room in his house. I tried not to even question those intentions because they may have actually been genuine, but the point is, in my mind I was relying on a man and not on my Father – the one Who had always been there to help me with absolutely no strings attached. After months of getting it worked on by different people, I prayed over that heater and God finally sent the *right* person. The mechanic simply replaced the motor for free and I haven't had another problem with that unit since! You see, God was my Provider all along, and I needed to go through that difficult time to remember it. Your Father is always your Provider – not a man. Make no mistake about it; although He may send a wonderful man as an earthly extension of His love for you, don't confuse the sustenance of your soul's desire or think that a man can do more for you than the true Lover of your soul – Jesus. It is clear what we must do. Remember,

> *What . . . the Lord your God ask[s] of you . . . to*
> *fear the Lord your God, to walk in all his ways,*
> *to love him, to serve the Lord your God with all*
> *your heart and with all your soul, and to observe*
> *the Lord's commands and decrees that . . . [are]*
> *for your own good.*
> *Deuteronomy 10:12-13 NIV*

The point is, no man can give you what Jesus can, and you really shouldn't expect him to. There is no other provider like Him. Remember the questions from chapter one? Now ask yourself the main question again – this time, take time to do some deep soul searching. Why do you want to get married? With all of the spiritual and self help books you have probably already read, including this one, don't forget to read the actual Word, God's Word. What does He say about you, about your future? In order to grow, you have to know what He says and you have to develop that much-needed relationship with Him. His Word is the best medicine for an ailing heart, weak spirit, or confused mind. God knew you and what you would need before the foundation of the world. And the answer to your needs is all in *that* Book – the Bible.

> *Therefore I tell you, do not worry about your life,*
> *what you will eat or drink; or about your body, what*
> *you will wear. Is not life more important than food,*
> *and the body more important than clothes? Look at*
> *the birds of the air; they do not sow or reap or store*
> *away in barns and yet your heavenly Father feeds*
> *them. Are you not much more valuable than they?*
> *Who of you by worrying can add a single hour to*
> *his life? . . . O you of little faith . . . Your heavenly*
> *Father knows [what you need]. But seek first his*
> *kingdom and his righteousness, and all these things*
> *will be given to you as well. Therefore do not worry*
> *about tomorrow, for tomorrow will worry about*
> *itself. Each day has enough trouble of its own.*
> *Matthew 6:25-28, 30b, 32b-34 NIV*

God uses everyday situations to remind us that He knows exactly what we need and when we need it. I can remember a rough day when I was really tired and felt under-appreciated. After going to the supermarket, the cashier told me that I had won my choice of a ham or a turkey for the Easter holiday. Well that really was a big deal for me because I had never won much of anything before. For me, it happened at the right time because of how I was feeling. God knew exactly what I needed and when. I wore a smile the whole evening – not because I had won the turkey, but because at that moment, I knew that God was paying attention to everything I needed. I truly had a place in His heart. I actually felt it!

Chapter 4

What Has God Promised You?

Has God promised you something? By the very nature of the question, there's already an expectation. The Lord has set a plan in motion. If you don't know what your promise is, or you simply have not yet spoken to God about one, this chapter is definitely for you. A large part of your journey toward your appointed time means having destined and momentary prayers *and* praise. God *will* present very specific words you ought to say to yourself in prayer. When that happens, at that very moment, you have to pray. It is not because God needs to hear it. It is because you need to hear yourself say it; God needs you to confess it so that He can act on it.

These prayers put you and God on one accord – pressing toward that mark. How does one get to this point – the point where you are in such a connection with the Lord that He speaks to you constantly and guides your prayers? Simply put, you really must take the time to commune with Him on a more consistent basis – keep Him first in your daily decisions and prayer life and also at the forefront of all of your relationships. The Bible lends us many examples of how imperfect people were still loved and used by the Lord simply because they had very open and honest relationships with Him.

The books of 1st and 2nd Samuel are perfect examples of how God will make a promise and see it through to the end, without hesitation and despite the faultiness of a person's character. In 1st Samuel, David's exile was not only about building his strength and endurance, it was about building a lasting and trusting covenant relationship with God. That's what a promise is – the building blocks of a covenant relationship. Right now you might feel like you're in your own exile period. If so, then bless God for it! Don't curse it.

This is your time, your period of fellowship with the Lord. This is your time of character building and actualization of future promises (the process of realizing, understanding, and then accepting the promises set for your life). Perhaps it will take the frustration of your singleness or your situation to catapult you into developing your eyes toward God's promise – His will for your life. For me, past exile periods always led to periods of pain, and it was out of that pain that God's repositioning of my life and purpose became crystal clear. Presently, His promises still reign as a constant and precious quench to the thirsty parts of my spirit. This could not have possibly developed without that personal relationship that I have been blessed to have with Him.

When you believe in the covenant that He has made with you, you truly begin to understand and value your worth – knowing who and Whose you are. When we fail to believe in God's promise, it usually stems from our own lack in knowing who we are. Before God's promise, David was a shepherd boy who followed flocks. After God's promise was revealed to David, that he was to now lead God's people, he removed himself for prayer. More importantly, remember that after God made David king, David's heart was still focused on taking care of God's business.

After the king was settled in his palace and the
Lord had given him rest from all his enemies
around him, he said to Nathan the prophet, 'Here
I am living in a palace of cedar, while the ark
of God remains in a tent.' Nathan replied to the
king, 'Whatever you have in mind, go ahead and
do it, For the Lord is with you.'
2 Samuel 7:1-3 NIV

Although David could have relished in his new title as king, immediately afterwards he thinks of how he could still please God – he wondered what unfinished business of the Lord's he could complete. After Nathan reveals God's words to David, he is still compelled to take time and go before the Lord for himself. If you are in or as you get into that sweet communion with Him, you will come to terms with understanding that God's words are true and they are lasting just as they were to David:

Then King David went in and sat before the Lord,
and he said: 'Who am I, O Sovereign Lord, and
what is my family, that you have brought me this
far? And as if this were not enough in your sight,
O Sovereign Lord, you have also spoken about
the future of the house of your servant.'... 'O
Sovereign Lord, you are God! Your words are
trustworthy, and you have promised these good
things to your servant.'
2 Samuel 7:18-19a, 28 NIV

There are two major truths that we can learn from the above

scriptures. For one thing, continue to plant and harvest seeds in light of taking care of God's business even after He reveals truths about your dream of becoming a wife. *He* must come first. Secondly, go before the Lord often to receive a direct word from Him. Confirmation through others is truly a beautiful thing, but when you allow your spirit to personally connect with God, there is nothing like it in the world. For many of you, a bond with God must be nurtured and set in place long before the title of wife ever comes. There is nothing wrong with that. In 2 Samuel 7:18 (NIV), David is referred to as King David and rightfully so. When he receives that title, he had already put in sacrificial time going earnestly before the Lord. He did not wait for the title of *king* to do so. And the same goes for you; you cannot wait for the title of *Mrs.* to go before the Lord with your whole heart and pray on behalf of your husband. Bishop Thomas Wesley Weeks, Sr. said it best: "You don't wait until you have the title in order to walk in your authority. A title only confirms it."

> "Do not ask the Lord to guide your footsteps if you're not willing to move your feet."
>
> (Joyce Meyer)

When in prayer, go peacefully before the Lord and ask what you will. Try not to go to God in anger to make your requests known. I say *try* because it will not always be easy, but think about how you would feel if your child came to you – with an attitude nonetheless – and made demands for anything. How would you feel? What would be your immediate response? Would the word *disrespect* come to mind? Try to remember that when your feelings of loneliness and fear feel like they are going to overtake you; those feelings do pass in time.

Part Two

Persevere by Following the Pilot's Plan
Through Prayer, Patience, and Poise

Read your Word for revelation....
Your situations are mirrored by the
many women of the Bible.

Chapter 5

You Cannot Appoint Your Own Seat

*D*on't let anyone or anything rob you of God's promise. Your royal seat was already appointed to you. Verbally declare the promise that God made to you, because "out of the abundance of the heart, the mouth speaketh" (Matt. 12:34b KJV). Repeated verbal confirmation is the key to sealing the deal of that promise. Verbal confirmation precedes the physical manifestation of what will take place – when it is a promise from the Lord. This is why we learn very early in our Christian walk to guard our tongue, for there is power in it – the power of life and death. Make no mistake about it; there are often serious repercussions when greed, envy, or even haste supersedes the gifts and promises of God.

After David, King of Israel, had anointed his own son, Solomon as king, there were thieves who were eager to steal David's reign while he was on his deathbed. David had already taken an oath to Bathsheba, his wife saying,

> . . . *'As surely as the Lord lives, who has delivered*
> *me out of every trouble, I will surely carry out*
> *today what I swore to you by the Lord, the God of*

Israel: Solomon your son shall be king after me,
and he will sit on my throne in my place. '
1 Kings 1:29-30 NIV

The city reverberated with cheering as the royal officials came to congratulate King David on the appointment of Solomon as king. At the same time, the *false* king Adonijah, was holding what he thought was his anticipatory celebration feast (1 Kings 1:41-53). How embarrassed he must have been to stand at his own falsified victory feast, which ironically almost became his last meal. The feast that was once fit for a king was abruptly interrupted by the celebratory appointment of the chosen king. Appointing yourself in any area without God's approval can ultimately lead to spiritual and emotional suicide or worse yet – the delaying of God's promise.

Do you really know just how valuable your hand and fellowship in marriage is within God's third dimensional plan? You see, most of us are so earthly, we cannot conceptualize that our unions are more important than wedding dresses, houses with picket fences, 2.5 kids, vacation homes, and retirement plans. For a great many of us, God needs us to understand that our unions extend far beyond what and how we feel – their importance supersedes our days on earth. Take President Barack Obama for example. The multiracial union of his parents, influential rearing by his grandparents, and the public displays of affection within a healthy marriage to his wife and best friend Michelle, was a major spark behind his winning campaign slogans, *Change* and *Yes We Can*. One of you could be just the generational healing your entire family has been waiting for. Another one of you might mother and someday breastfeed the child who will grow into the scientist that will break the code to provide a vaccine for breast cancer.

Do you believe it's possible? Understand that marriage and cleaving is deeper than the world has been able to explain. And right, wrong, or indifferent – as a woman, you have more power to wield the decisions and directions of men than you think you do or are given credit for.

Focus once again on 1 Kings 2:13-23 for a moment. King Solomon's brother Adonijah, son of Haggith, believed for certain that Solomon would not dare refuse his own mother's (Bathsheba) request. So believing, Adonijah asked her to plead a sneaky request on his own behalf. He knew that if he could get one of King David's companions, Abishag, to marry him, he would gain inroads to the throne that he had lost to Solomon. Adonijah needed to benefit from the kingdom's love and respect for Solomon's mother, a trusted woman. He would then in turn, win the hand of the late king's concubine. That would give him indirect power and connection to kingship. After Solomon heard of Adonijah's cunning use of Bathsheba, King Solomon recognized the request for what it was, a conspiracy to once again chip away at their father's throne. He ordered that Adonijah's life be "struck down" (1 Kings 2:25).

Look at this example spiritually. Perhaps men won't really lose their lives in the natural for misusing your relationship with God for their own selfish benefits. But they *may* lose their credibility with other men, God's favor, or His patient ear - an ear that was once bent in their direction when they prayed and trusted in God's direction for themselves. Just as Adonijah kept a watchful eye on the relationship Bathsheba had with her son Solomon, there are also those men that are watchful of you and your relationship with *the* King. Many of them can see God's hand upon your life. Perhaps there is an aura about you, one that does resonate with a shimmer or sparkle of God's personal relationship, connection, and communication with you. If you should ever become weak and unable to see any plot against you, you could easily fall prey to the evil and wicked deeds of others. To prevent this, in all things ask God to instill in you His godly knowledge, wisdom, and discernment. Then, learn to look beyond what is obvious – that which is only visible with the naked eye.

Chapter 6

Learn to Look Beyond the Obvious

What opportunity has He given you to become a blessing in the lives of others? Is your husband the *only* thing that's on your mind? Be careful! Heavily dwelling on your husband or any other promise God has made to you could be considered an act of disobedience as well as faithlessness, because complete trust in God means absolute trust in His timing as well.

The story of Ruth and Naomi is one of an uncompromising bond – a noteworthy example of God's indirect intervention while having His credited visible presence in the meeting between Ruth and her beloved Boaz. Make no mistake about it; Ruth did want a husband – not only for herself but she wanted someone to help her take care of her beloved mother-in-law, Naomi. At first, it was a little disconcerting that Naomi seemed to have had a little more faith and concern in God's delivery of a husband for Ruth than she did on her own. Nevertheless, Ruth's overall concern for Naomi later worked in Ruth's favor.

> *Then Naomi said to her two daughters-in-law,*
> *'Go back each of you, to your mother's home.*
> *May the Lord show kindness to you, as you have*

shown to your dead and to me. May the Lord
grant that each of you will find rest in the home of
another husband. . . . Return home, my daughters'
. . . At this they wept again. . . . Ruth clung to her.
'Look,' said Naomi, 'your sister-in law is going
back to her people and her gods. Go back with
her.' But Ruth replied, 'Don't urge me to leave
you or turn back from you. Where you go, I will
go, and where you stay I will stay. Your people
will be my people and your God will be my God.'
Ruth 1:8-16 NIV

Later, Ruth and Naomi came together in agreement for God to move in Ruth's favor. Not only was it their combined faith that moved God, it was also Ruth's obedience, determination, and faithfulness in taking care of her mother-in-law. Although Ruth was indeed clear in decreeing the desires of her heart (a husband), she was also selfless in her commitment to Naomi. Her husband had died and she was without children. In the days and times of the Old Testament, it was customary for young women to have already been married with children by the time they had reached Ruth's age. I'm sure she probably had her moments when she thought of her own situation as a hopeless one, bellowing questions like, "Why me?" or "Will I ever marry again, Lord?"

There is no mention of those thoughts in the Bible because her ultimate obedience was better than her sacrifice. Perhaps she trusted God so much that she dare not go back on the commitment she made to Naomi. Ruth was prepared to follow Naomi anywhere until death.

> *'Where you die I will die, and there I will be*
> *buried. May the Lord deal with me be it ever so*
> *severely, if anything but death separates*
> *you and me.' When Naomi realized that Ruth was*
> *determined to go with her, she stopped*
> *urging her.*
> *Ruth 1:17-18 NIV*

Now that's commitment! Do you have this type of commitment to the Lord - the type that says your obedience is better than your sacrifice? Ruth had mentally prepared herself for whatever God's will was for her life. Her vow to take care of her mother-in-law was fascinatingly stronger than her desire to marry again. Has God asked you to shift your attention off yourself and channel your energies and focus onto something more pressing than your own desires? Ponder these questions. Have you been ignoring God's promptings? Are you delaying your own promises, the ones He has made to you? The end result for Ruth's faithfulness paid off in her favor.

> **"You cannot reap the benefits of the anointing in selfishness. The anointing is rooted in love."**
>
> (Creflo Dollar)

Now focus your attention on Naomi's bitterness and lack of faith in God:

> *So the two women went on until they came to*
> *Bethlehem. When they arrived in Bethlehem,*
> *The whole town was stirred because of them,*
> *and the women exclaimed, 'Can this be Naomi?'*
> *'Don't call me Naomi,' she told them. 'Call me*

*Mara, because the Almighty has made my life
very bitter. I went away full, but the Lord has
brought me back empty. Why call me Naomi?
The Lord has afflicted me; the Almighty has
brought misfortune upon me.'
Ruth 1:19-21 NIV*

It is more than probable that when the townspeople saw Naomi and Ruth, their surprise and amazement was not only due to seeing Naomi after such a long time, it was also out of disbelief at how bad she looked and how unhappily she came back into town. Naomi left her homeland when it was in a famine. However, before she returned, the famine had lifted and the people were grateful and cheerful. When Naomi returned with her frowns, wrinkles, and poor attitude, she naturally became the talk of everyone.

Exuding bitterness, or having mannerisms that portray that only animosity surrounds you, pushes people away. Although you may be in the midst of trouble and your words may be a little stifled and without melody, your tattered emotions, lamentable gestures, and faltering attitude may say something much worse. Do they reflect God? God does not deserve our shifting of blame, our murmuring, or our complaining.

Naomi allowed her present challenges to cloud her memory; she had forgotten everything that God had done for her up until that point. All she could think about was her loss. She had lost her will to live and her hope in the future because her present looked so different from anything she had ever hoped for herself. Is there anything you can learn from Naomi's fault-finding attitude? How many of you have walked a mile in the fault-finding shoes of Naomi? Did murmuring and complaining ever change God's mind or get Him to move quicker on your behalf?

As the story goes on, because Ruth was obedient to the vow she had made, the Lord more than favored her. Not only was she blessed, but Naomi reaped from the overflow of Ruth as well. Naomi was rewarded because of the charge God had placed in her life – the direction and guidance of Ruth. What are the charges (the responsibilities) God has placed in your life? What tasks has He given you?

Meditate on Ruth's direction and her focus for a moment. She was much more preoccupied with taking care of Naomi than she was with getting her own prayers answered, her own needs met. Just as Ruth was asking for permission to glean in the fields behind the harvesters in order to provide food for herself and Naomi, God was making provisions for Ruth to meet Boaz, her husband, her future, her metaphoric opened window after a dismal closed door (Ruth 2:8 NIV). And suddenly, Boaz noticed her. As a matter of fact, he inquired about her as she was working. Ruth did *not* go out to initially find her husband; quite the contrary, she was much more focused on the charge she was given by the Lord. Ruth's relationship with Naomi could be named as one of the first indirect female ministries. Ruth's life of servant-hood and selflessness, her uncompromising walk with God, and her immovable faith mirrors so many of the ministries that God had placed in so many of our lives as we, too, wait for our Boaz.

Perhaps, unbeknown to her, Ruth was worshiping God through her servant-hood to Naomi. For such a time as this, many of us, too, have been called into service for the kingdom. And what an honor it is! If you cannot serve the Lord in *every* capacity to which He calls you, how do you intend to serve your husband in *any* capacity to which he calls you – needs you? Or, have you already made up in your mind that you will *not* serve Him when needed? In the times of the Old Testament, it was customary for the poor to work for what they needed rather than beg or merely look for handouts. The scriptures say that Ruth was tending to the fields in harvesting and gathering leftover grain when Boaz recognized her and inquired about who she was.

> *Boaz asked the foreman of his harvesters, 'Whose young woman is that?' The foreman replied, 'She is the Moabitess who came back from Moab with Naomi.' She said, 'Please let me glean and gather among the sheaves behind the harvesters.' She went into the field and has worked steadily from morning till now, except for a short rest in the shelter.'*
> *Ruth 2:5-7 NIV*

Even though Boaz knew of her financial state (her lack), he was more concerned with what filled her heart rather than her pockets. Ruth was focused, driven, and goal-oriented. She was pressing toward her mark – committed to honoring Naomi, committed to God's direction. What's more important about this scripture is that not only does it speak to Ruth's discipline, obedience, and focus; it also says something about her *perseverance* and *poise*. Ruth was more than aware of what she was capable of doing and what was beyond her limited power. How many of you are still more than willing to sit down and let God do all of the work, even that which you are more than capable of taking care of for yourselves? As God does His part to prepare us for our role within wifedom, there are a number of tasks He has set before us to take care of for ourselves. This too is all part of the process, and you cannot escape the process – it's what makes us who we are. It's all a very large part of the ministry.

From the moment Boaz saw Ruth, he was more than prepared, willing, and able to *cover* Ruth. You see, God knows exactly what you want *and* what you need. He was making provisions for Ruth behind the scenes even before marriage, even before the courtship.

> *So Boaz said to Ruth, 'My daughter, listen to me.*
> *Don't go and glean in another field and don't go*
> *away from here. Stay here with my servant girls.*
> *Watch the field where the men are harvesting, and*
> *follow along after the girls. I have told the men*
> *not to touch you. And whenever you are thirsty,*
> *go and get a drink from the water jars the men*
> *have filled.' At this, she bowed down with her*
> *face to the ground. She exclaimed, 'Why have I*
> *found such favor in your eyes that you notice me*
> *– a foreigner?'*
> *Ruth 2:8-10 NIV*

Ruth had not understood why Boaz would take notice of her or how she could have found such favor with him because she was a foreigner, an outsider. This is a spiritual translation of the manifestations in our own lives, symbolic to those of us who don't quite understand how we've come to walk into so many of the provisions and blessings that befall us. Many times we know that we don't even deserve such blessings. But His continued mercy, love, forgiveness, and patience are tied to the purpose that He has set before our lives. For the most part – *favor ain't fair*. We've all heard it, but how many of us truly understand it?

The favor that Ruth had found with the Lord and with Boaz is directly tied to her overall purpose and God's direction for her life. More importantly, it is the outcome of her inward faith and the onset of her outward promise (covenant) to Naomi, connected by a positive attitude through the test of her obedience. How many of us know how to tap into that kind of unlimited power of God – power which turns the heads of suitors, enemies, and other onlookers to command the attention of those in authority?

> *At mealtime, Boaz said to her, 'Come over here.*
> *Have some bread and dip it into the wine vinegar.'*
> *When she sat down with the harvesters, he offered*
> *her some roasted grain. She ate all she wanted and*
> *had some left over. As she got up to glean, Boaz*
> *gave orders to his men, 'Even if she gathers among*
> *the sheaves, don't embarrass her. Rather, pull out*
> *some stalks for her from the bundles and leave them*
> *for her to pick up, and don't rebuke her.'*
> *Ruth 2:14-16 NIV*

Ruth had presence! By humbling herself before the Lord, and without even trying, all provisions and blessings were laid at her feet by the most unlikely sources – her future husband and king. Now do you see why timing is everything? As Ruth continued to keep a good attitude, Boaz kept watch over her, at times even acknowledging her most positive attributes. Will your husband find you "gleaning" or will he find you grumbling and complaining as you wait for a hand out?

Chapter 7

Submissive Doesn't Mean Passive

*S*ometimes Christian women admit that they can never truly be submissive to a man. There really is a good reason for many of them admitting that they truly lack the understanding of its meaning. They look at it as a dirty word in a marriage from the female perspective. Becoming submissive to your husband is a respected attitude that does not include being *stepped on*, ignored, used, or ridiculed. Becoming submissive is unto the Lord – it's not about women losing power so that men can gain it. Quite the contrary, when God purposes the act, the person who is submissive is actually the one who is in control. Divert your attention to Queen Esther for a moment as an example of this.

The book of Esther speaks of a vengeful Persian king who preferred a quiet beauty from his wives, coupled with complete obedience to the rules of his kingdom's protocol. As a matter of fact, when King Xerxes' wife, Queen Vashti, refused his invitation "to display her beauty to the people and the nobles," she was actually stripped of her royal crown, faced banishment, and was denied access to her king from that moment on (Esther 1:11, 19 NIV). Her royal position was to be given to someone else out of fear that her defiance would spark other women to do the same against their husbands.

> *'According to law, what must be done to Queen*
> *Vashti?' he asked. 'She has not obeyed the*
> *command of King Xerxes. For the queen's*
> *conduct will become known to all the women,*
> *and so they will despise their husbands and say,*
> *"King Xerxes commanded Queen Vashti to be*
> *brought before him, but she would not come."*
> *'There will be no end of disrespect and discord.'*
> *Esther 1:15-18 NIV*

We will never know if a simple headache kept the queen from attending the party as requested by the king. But in all seriousness, it is hard to imagine – being stripped of your *queendom* and access to your own husband simply because you didn't feel like accompanying him to a business dinner. Think of the humiliation Queen Vashti must have felt.

Nevertheless, Vashti's defiance, disobedience, and strong will had cost her the status and position of a lifetime. This too is a lesson in itself because many times women emasculate their own husbands, boyfriends, brothers, and sons simply because they misunderstand the position of helpmate, for they lack clarity on their role as a partner or friend. Some women truly feel weak in their role because they are not called the head of the family. However, just because a woman is not the head does not mean she is necessarily the tail. What head can lead without the support, strength, and flexibility of the neck to which it is attached? Perhaps Queen Vashti saw herself as the *tail* instead of the *neck*. Perception changes everything. When more women see themselves as a viable support system in a relationship, then healthy dialogue about the role of a submissive wife can take place.

Without spending too much time on Vashti's issues, they really did serve to benefit another woman's success to save the lives of her people. From birth, so it seems, God had prepared Esther for her role as a wife but not just any wife – the wife of a very powerful king. Who is the Lord preparing you for? It was Esther's beloved cousin and guardian, Mordecai, who had adopted her after the death of her parents and raised her as his very own daughter. When it became time for King Xerxes to find yet another queen, it was Mordecai who made sure that Esther was safe even while part of the king's harem. Some would probably assume that Esther's stay in the harem was a humiliating one, but quite the contrary. Esther's entrance into the harem was all a part of God's plan, which was much larger than becoming a mere concubine. She had to spend countless months attending cleansing rituals and perfuming techniques to please the king.

> "Destiny is not left up to chance, but it is a matter of choice."
>
> (Bishop E. Bernard Jordan)

> *Before a girl's turn came to go in to King Xerxes, she had to complete twelve months of beauty treatments prescribed for the women, six months with oil of myrrh and six with perfumes and cosmetics. A girl would not return to the king unless he was pleased with her and summoned her by name. When the turn came for Esther to go to the king, she asked for nothing other than what Hegai, the king's eunuch who was in charge of the harem, suggested. And Esther won the favor of everyone who saw her.*
> *Esther 2:12-15 NIV*

How does Esther's situation, her months of *cleansing*, relate to the period of preparation you have attained under God's tutelage? Just like Esther, there are going to be days that the cleansing process feels more like pampering than work, and then there are other days that it will probably feel more like a boot camp type of experience than like a blessing in disguise. But in the end, Esther was the one the king preferred over all others. I cannot help but to believe that when God is finished cleansing you that perhaps your earthly king will prefer you to all others as well. But first God has to get you to a place where the right people (or person) will notice you without you even trying. There is a lesson in understanding how God operates in your favor.

Accept the fact that God will not just bestow the power of favor and authority upon you without teaching you how to operate in it. This is why I am a firm believer that the one who is submissive does indeed have control. However, the cleansing process is almost always about the instruction on how to handle your power with reverential fear, ease, and respect. This cleansing process is about the time you must put in with God so that He can build your character as an *appointed* queen like Esther instead of a backslidden concubine. Gaining access isn't that hard; maintaining it is a different story, especially when you've lost the anointing!

As you become *processed*, cleansed, and transformed into the woman God has destined you to become, many of you may have several opportunities in which to gain the trust of your earthly king. By using that trust, you could save him from his enemies or even hold up the mirror that causes him to see God's image within his own reflection long before he actually marries you. When Mordecai uncovered the guard's conspiracy to kill the king, it presented the perfect opportunity for Esther to gain the king's trust and save Mordecai's life at the same time. Just like Queen Esther, your window of opportunity to minister into *his* life begins with the moment you see him and he hears your voice, not when he asks, "Will you marry me?"

Although submissive, without being passive, Esther found the most effective way to get her husband's attention without getting ignored and without being disrespectful. Forget those *How to* magazines, Esther is an excellent teacher of the three steps in highly effective communication skills with a man: (1) learn as much as possible about him which means you must listen to his wants, desires, fears, confusions, etc., (2) gain his trust, which means you have to know him better than any other person, and (3) appeal to his sense of reason because if it doesn't make sense to him, he will not envision himself with full participation.

The third chapter of the book of Esther reveals that just as Haman devised a plot to destroy the Jews, there are those that will stop at nothing to see that your future husband is also destroyed – his name, his livelihood, and his happiness. And his enemies may go to extra lengths to do so. Haman not only hated the Jews, he wanted to see all of them pay for the offenses of one man – Mordecai. The anger went from being one of personal hatred mainly toward one man to that of wrath and annihilation of all of Mordecai's people, the Jews.

Your husband's enemies are also your enemies. The successful plot to destroy your partner is also one against you and your family. Knowing, believing, then acting against this is only half the battle. Esther's call on her life was to save her people, but Mordecai had to remind her of the authority she had in the house of the king. Mordecai also played an instrumental and pivotal role in the plan to save the lives of the Jews as well. His role and position in Esther's life metaphorically mirrors the Lord's promptings in our own lives. It was

Mordecai's distress that initially alerted Esther about what she had to do; the role she played in saving her people.

> *Hathach went back and reported to Esther what*
> *Mordecai had said. Then she instructed him*
> *to say to Mordecai, 'All the king's officials and the*
> *people of the royal provinces know that for any man*
> *or woman who approaches the king in the inner court*
> *without being summoned the king has but one law:*
> *that he be put to death. The only exception to this is*
> *for the king to extend the gold scepter to him and spare*
> *his life. But thirty days have passed since I was called*
> *to go to the king.' When Esther's words were reported*
> *to Mordecai, he sent back this answer: 'Do not think*
> *that because you are in the king's house you alone of*
> *all the Jews will escape. For if you remain silent at*
> *this time, relief and deliverance for the Jews will arise*
> *from another place, but you and your father's family*
> *will perish. And who knows but that you have come to*
> *royal position for such a time as this?'*
> *Esther 4:9-14 NIV*

Often, after realizing the call on their lives, many women take for granted their very position to positively affect change as instructed by God. Many believe that God's will is not possibly going to get done if not by their hands or help. Quite the contrary, fear, doubt, unbelief, disobedience, pride, and slothfulness might hinder the blessings of the disobedient one, but God's will is still going to come to pass. If God has called you and has awarded you the opportunity to be a blessing in someone's life, remember that He is so sovereign that the blessing

"By faith you have to go into some things that have the *potential* to take you out. You have to believe by faith. Believe God for your vision, your dream, your business, your marriage. Why can't you just believe God? Go to the enemies' camp believing God by faith. This is no time to be still."

(Bishop Gilbert Coleman)

is two-fold, meant for you as well as the other person. It's not a mistake that He wants to use you. Think of it as another opportunity for character growth and development – one more rung on the ladder of wifedom. Esther not only teaches that *obedience is better than sacrifice*, but that one can still have favor while feeling fearful.

There is a man out there who needs you to save his spiritual life or his career, guard his prayers or even unmask his weaknesses, hold his hand or simply to protect his heart. But if you *will not* do it, as important as it is, it will still get done, even if He has to use the hand of another. Unfortunately, this is how so many women lose out on their opportunity to show themselves as a helpmate. From beginning to end, there is work in wifedom!

In the end, Esther did adhere to the petition of her beloved guardian Mordecai.

> Then Esther sent this reply to Mordecai: 'Go, gather together all the Jews who are in Susa, and fast for me. Do not eat or drink for three days, night or day. I and my maids will fast as you do. When this is

done, I will go to the king, even though it is against
the law. And if I perish, I perish.'
Esther 4:15-16 NIV

And even after agreeing to put her own life on the line, Esther still knew she needed to fast and go before the presence of God. She would have been foolish not to. Conversing with God during life-changing events is at the pinnacle of making it through successfully. In the end, as Joyce Meyer would say, Esther "did it afraid." She put her royal robes on her back, her life on the line, and stepped into the king's inner court. Even though God is not mentioned by name in Esther, the events recorded in the book can hardly be considered coincidental. Everything from Esther's rearing by her cousin Mordecai to her ability to bend the ear of her husband King Xerxes is an important part of God's Word because of the release of His power in everything. In Esther's walk nothing happened, just as nothing ever does, without His knowledge or His consent. To set the redemption in motion, the Lord caused Xerxes to experience insomnia for,

That night the king could not sleep; so he ordered the
book of the chronicles, the record of his reign, to be
brought in and read to him. It was found recorded
there that Mordecai had exposed Bigthana and Teresh
. . . who had conspired to assassinate King Xerxes.
'What honor and recognition has Mordecai received
for this?' the king asked. 'Nothing has been done for
him,' his attendants answered.
Esther 6:1-3 NIV

And who do you think caused the king to lay awake that night? Was it a mere coincidence that Mordecai's recorded heroism was exposed to the king only hours before he was to be hanged by Haman, a powerful enemy of the Jews? This too, is a lesson in itself. Often we make the mistake of looking for God's stamp of approval or confirmation that He really wants us to move onward in a decision *after* He has already told us what to do and that He is in it with us. Confirmation is not the culprit; it is lack of faith that is dangerous. Many times, like Esther, we must act quickly when hearing from God. The window of opportunity is only open for so long – a set time. What might have happened if Esther hadn't acted as quickly upon Mordecai's request? The story may have been written of her demise rather than her success.

No one but God could have orchestrated such perfect timing. While the king had Mordecai's great act of chivalry read to him, Haman was approaching the king's court in hopes of receiving his blessing to hang Mordecai. But in a vain attempt to have the king honor or pay homage to him, Haman unknowingly helped the king to plan a show of respect to his number one enemy – Mordecai. His generous self-edifying plans spoken to the king were:

> *'For the man the king delights to honor, have them*
> *bring a royal robe the king has worn and a horse the*
> *kind has ridden, one with a royal crest placed on its*
> *head. Robe the man the king delights to honor, and*
> *[have them] lead him on the horse through the city*
> *streets, proclaiming before him, 'This is what is done*
> *for the man the king delights to honor!' [Much to*
> *Haman's surprise, the king answered] 'Go at once*
> *. . . get the robe and the horse and do just as you*
> *have suggested for Mordecai the Jew, who sits at*
> *the king's gate. Do not neglect anything you have*

recommended.'
Esther 6:7b-10 NIV

Who else but God could make your enemy your footstool? Mordecai had no idea any of this was happening. As Bishop Mark Hanby says, this is a very simple case of "one situation, two things happening." All Mordecai could do was sit, wonder, pray, and hope Esther was getting through to King Xerxes. His communication with her was truly limited. How might this mirror your own situation? Has God ever instructed you to focus on one area while He dealt with a completely different concern? Were you struck by the inability to see how or if either situation was ever going to turn out in your favor?

Well, the story of Esther should help you breathe a little easier. God has been handling both sides of the chessboard and winning *every* match since the beginning of time. No matter how gray the situation while dealing with it, picture the Lord on both the inside of it with you and on the outside of it, controlling both at the same time. No matter how things turn out, you are bound to be the winner when He is on your side.

Esther's submissive nature and acts of obedience are examples of her strength portrayed through God's favor. I can remember a time in my own life when God instructed me to "Be still" when I wanted so much to move away from a situation – and to wash my hands of a friendship I felt was stagnant. All the while He was telling me to be still, I felt my spirit being driven to pray without ceasing. It took some time for me to understand that more of God's power was exercised in my acts of submission and obedience. My pompous need to control the situation almost led to my sacrificing His favor. So many of us need to stop worrying about how our situations may look in the eyes of others and start concerning ourselves with aligning our spiritual ear with God's discerning voice! Allow His will to play out.

His will was evident in the putting to death of Haman and the giving of his estate to Mordecai. Esther, doing her part,

> *. . . again pleaded with the king . . . Then the king extended the gold scepter to Esther and she arose and stood before him. 'If it pleases the king,' she said, 'and if he regards me with favor and thinks it is the right thing to do, and if he is pleased with me, let an order be written overruling the dispatches that Haman son of Hammedatha, the Agagite, devised and wrote to destroy the Jews in all the king's provinces. For how can I bear to see disaster fall on my people? How can I bear to see the destruction of my family?'*
> *Esther 8:3a, 4-6 NIV*

Esther never nagged, raised her voice, or tried to emasculate the king to get what she wanted. All of the strength she needed was in her acts of humility, her walk of faith, and her obedience before the Lord, the One who developed her character. By far, submission is not about weakness; on the contrary, it is merely a matter of casting your care before the Lord, recognizing that true acts of faith are evident in your daily submission as you carry out God's will, even when you cannot make sense of it. Romans 8:28 (NIV) reminds us "And we know that in all things God works for the good of those who love him, who have been called according to his purpose." The power of submission means giving up the desire to know how every piece of the puzzle will come together: it is trusting in the Lord that it will all work out in your favor.

Chapter 8

Know Your Worth

$\mathscr{B}$e honest, have you ever compared yourself to any aspect of another woman – size, shape, looks, careers, bank accounts, marital status? For me, the question shouldn't be *"have you ever compared yourself?"* as much as it should be *"how often have you compared yourself to other women?"* But the more I come to understand God's love for me and that I am truly *fearfully and wonderfully made* in His image, the more I have come to understand that heavy judgment and a critical nature toward myself is also heavy judgment against God, for it was He who created me.

Women have compared themselves to others since the beginning of time itself. Even in the famous story in Genesis, Leah is compared to her sister Rachel.

> *Now Laban had two daughters; the name of the*
> *older was Leah, and the name of the younger was*
> *Rachel. Leah had weak eyes, but Rachel was*
> *lovely in form, and beautiful.*
> *Genesis 29:16-17 NIV*

Now, the specifics of the story never directly say that Leah compared *herself* to Rachel. However, imagine the situation of one having a younger sister whose form was considered lovely *and* beautiful, while the reference to the older sister was that her eyes were weak or delicate. Do you think the words weak and delicate were meant as flattery? The comparison for Leah probably did not start with her. Everyone in her village, including family, most likely had a hand in that. Also, imagine the strain this must have placed on the sisters' relationship with one another. Leah's eyes were weak because she could not see her worth pass her appearance in the mirror. If the eyes are the mirror to the soul, then Leah's eyes told a story of fear, desperation, doubt, and maybe even a little depression.

We run across women like Leah all the time – at work, the gym, the market. Some of us may even encounter her in the image looking back at us in the mirror. The Leahs of the world come in all ethnicities, shapes, and sizes, from the unemployed to those with high-powered executive positions; some are single, others have husbands, and some even keep a string of Mr. Right Nows on speed dial because being alone is always their last option. The point is this; there is no cookie cutter mold or master formula for explaining the 21st Century version of the Biblical Leah. For many of us, she exists within our close circles one way or another. Uncovering Leah's issues is not only vital for the building of our own character, it is also crucial that you understand who she is and why she hurts so that you do not ever adopt her baggage – or bring it into your own Promised Land.

> *Jacob was in love with Rachel and said, 'I'll work for you seven years in return for your younger daughter Rachel.' Laban said, 'It's*

better that I give her to you than to some other
man. Stay here with me.' So Jacob served seven
years to get Rachel, but they seemed like only a
few days to him because of his love for her.
Genesis 29:18-20 NIV

Poor Leah – seeing Jacob work for several years for her father
Laban in order to receive her little sister's hand in marriage instead
of hers. As a matter of fact, it was Jacob's idea to work for Laban for
seven years before he would ever wed Rachel! Seven years! Many
women are afraid to ask a man to *wait* seven months, but this man
volunteered his commitment!

If you know the story of Leah and Rachel, then you also know
about Laban's plot to marry off his first-born daughter before the
younger one. If you understand anything about karma, then you know
that Laban's lies and trickery were merely the counteractions to Jacob's
theft of his brother Esau's birthright (Genesis 27). Laban's lies and
Jacob's schemes are the indirect connection to Leah's insecurities. Of
all the discussions about the possible rivalry between the two sisters,
very rarely is there discussion about Leah's hand in Laban's plan.

Then Jacob said to Laban, 'Give me my wife.
My time is completed, and I want to lie with her.'
So Laban brought together all the people of the
place and gave a feast. But when evening came,
he took his daughter Leah and gave her to Jacob,
and Jacob lay with her.
Genesis 29: 21-23 NIV

There had to have been a conversation between Laban and his

daughter Leah in order for this scheme to work. I often wonder if there was any reluctance on her part at all or whether she cried tears of joy as she embraced her father for coming up with the plan in the first place. Nevertheless, Leah swallowed any ounce of pride and self-restraint she may have had, dressed herself in her sister's bridal clothes, hid underneath the heavy veil, and married Jacob in the name of God and with the stolen identity of her sister.

Get a mental picture of Leah under this heavy veil for a moment. One symbolic purpose of the bride wearing a veil is to indicate that the woman *is* covered – her insecurities, fears, mistakes, and even her past is covered. When today's bride is uncovered by the groom at the end of the ceremony, in front of guests and witnesses, this becomes a symbolic revelation to everyone that he is prepared to take on all that was once covered and protected by her father – her Heavenly Father as well as her earthly one. Unknowingly, once Jacob consummated his marriage to Leah, he also uncovered many of her insecurities, her lies, her fears, and her selfish behaviors.

Some may ask why Leah would do all of this. The answer really is clear. Leah did this for the same reasons as so many *modern* women who would rather plan a pregnancy than to let go of a failing relationship. Or, for the reason why others would ruin another woman's credibility at work to underhandedly steal her promotion. Or, the classic act of those *friends* who make daily attempts to speak negatively about the love relationships of their sister-friends because of their jealousy and lack of faith in God's personal direction and His ordered steps for their *own* lives. If Leah truly knew God on an intimate level, she probably would not have readily doubted herself, stolen her sister's position as wife, or changed her identity for the sake of trading in the handle of Miss for Mrs. Remember, it's not your time until God says it's your time.

Now although she had gotten the husband she was looking for, Leah never *really* had Jacob because his love was always with Rachel, someone who knew her worth as did everyone else who knew her. Leah's fight was a daily one – against her husband's neglect, her sister's value, and her constant battle with low self-esteem. Jesus paid the ultimate price for the value of our salvation and personal relationship with God; He paid the price with His own life. When any of us puts on the *lenses of Leah* and devalues our self-worth, it is the epitome of standing at the feet of the King while He is on Calvary and turning our hearts and spirits away from Him. Everything He did, He did it for us, and failing to love yourself is also failure to recognize His love for you. God has told you just how much He truly loves you.

> *For those God foreknew he also predestined to be*
> *conformed to the likeness of his Son, that he might*
> *be the firstborn among many brothers. And those*
> *he predestined, he also called; those he called, he*
> *also justified; those he justified, he also glorified.*
> *Romans 8:29-30 NIV*

Is Leah your mirrored image? If so, change gears and shift into a new direction before Leah's reflection is looking back at you.

Sometimes we think that because we're beautiful and saved, we are a great catch. We often wonder why we are without a husband. After all, many of us have wonderful jobs or careers, substantial bank accounts, warm and inviting smiles, and pleasant personalities. Often times we daydream and wonder, "Is this a nightmare? What did I do wrong?" Stop right there! If a woman fails to recognize her self-value and worth, with or without a mate, the process of leaving and cleaving becomes complicated and extremely difficult. Thinking of singleness as a punishment is definitely not God's intention. The below scripture expounds on a previous one and gives clear instructions.

> *I would like you to be free from concern. An*
> *unmarried man is concerned about the Lord's*
> *affairs – how he can please the Lord. . . . An*
> *unmarried woman or virgin is concerned about*
> *the Lord's affairs: Her aim is to be devoted to the*
> *Lord in both body and spirit. . . . I am saying this*
> *for your own good, not to restrict you, but that*
> *you may live in a right way in undivided devotion*
> *to the Lord.*
> *1 Corinthians 7:32, 34a, 35 NIV*

While single, your focus ought to be on the Lord and how you can be effective within His kingdom with your ministry, good works, and service unto others. Believe that you are worth more than what you've had in the past or what ails you in the present. While your heart and spirit are focused on God's work instead of the works of the flesh that leaves room for the Lord to do what He has to do. Think on Dr. Mark Hanby's motto, "One situation, two things happening." Some daily meditation on this principle might actually be helpful. You might be beautiful, patient, kind, and even pleasing to the sight of the naked eye, but only God can uncover those blemishes in character that no one else can or would want to see – even the ones that are deeply hidden from you.

God is so awesome. He knows exactly what has to change in us in order to meet a higher standard for the king we've asked him for. Many of the issues and baggage that we struggle with has to first be revealed and then cast away long before our husbands can be revealed to us. Psalm 84:11 (NIV) states, "For the Lord God is a sun and shield; the Lord bestows favor and honor; no good thing does he withhold from those whose walk is blameless." The Lord is not keeping anything from you to cause you pain; on the contrary, this period of purging is a necessary step so that He can get you one step closer to what you have asked Him for. Aren't you striving to be part of that statistical 50% of successful marriages? Then, "Cast your cares on the Lord and he will sustain you; he will never let the righteous fall" (Psalm 55:22 NIV).

Near my home, there was a house that stood alone and was not lived in for about two years or so. The owners tried to sell the house in its then present condition, to no avail. Those owners probably thought the house would sell almost immediately because it was a very large house in a beautifully well-established neighborhood. Usually, real estate spoke for itself in this particular area. But that was not the case with this house. They changed realtors, even planted flowers to offer more curb appeal. Still, nothing happened. Then, they must have realized that drastic changes were necessary. Eventually they performed a lot of cosmetic work on the house, both inside and out. New real estate brokers were brought in. The owners altered the price, changed the wiring, and put a new roof on. Now it was ready.

At first, I did not understand why I was so drawn toward watching the process of this house's renewal, why it was so appealing to me. After two years and some renovations, it sold; then I understood. The transformation of that house mirrored much of the transformation God was taking me though as well.

> "Anyone can start but only the finishers are successful!"
>
> (Armando Montelongo)

Although I thought I was ready for marriage and the responsibility of caring for someone else, I was unaware that the Lord still had a "CAUTION – GOD AT WORK" sign hanging around me. How does this transformation relate to yours? Have you knowingly started your process with God yet? Stop looking to label God's process with your own stamp of approval. Deep down, you already know that's not quite the way things work. When are you going to ready yourself and completely surrender to His will? Well, at least you know one thing – God is the One that has all of the time in the world. How much time do you have?

Part Three

Proceed with Power and Praise –
Posture Yourself for This Wifedom Position

*"The oak tree is in the acorn.
Respect the seed; you'll see the fruit."*
Bishop T. D. Jakes

Chapter 9

Preach to Your Promise but Minister to that Man

Many single women have platonic male friends. On a healthy level we usually refer to them as our brothers. But why is it that so many single women find it necessary to look for and investigate every little detail, each right, wrong, or indifferent principle in their male friends, mates, brothers, and acquaintances? Remember, men are wired differently; they process information on a level most women find perplexing. Unfortunately for us, many men are generalized as womanizers who are not looking to find a healthy relationship. Some women feel that they must always be on alert. To some extent, that is necessary. However, specifically looking for a man's issues can become problematic. One reason is, God will reveal all in due time. Every man that you meet does not have to register on your Richter scale of the husbandry speedometer.

It's important that you understand that the search for his issues just might be a byproduct of looking through the wrong eye – a misunderstanding of his role and purpose in befriending you. Secondly, your focus on him takes the focus off where it really belongs – strengthening your relationship with God and allowing Him to reveal your own character flaws to *you*. Don't overlook the obvious, but the bottom line is that He will reveal what you need to know at the appointed and appropriate time when you are disciplined and mature enough to understand and handle what you're seeing. Instead of placing labels on a man's demeanor and forcing yourself into figuring out something that only God is privy to, try praying for him and emulating the love, compassion, and fellowship that makes up Christ-like behavior.

When you finally accept and realize that there are men in your life that may fall short of God's direction, or who are not saved, or who plainly need a word from God, it is then that you should channel that finger-pointing energy and nagging spirit into diligent prayer. There is nothing that quite moves God like that of a praying spirit. If there are days you would rather be fleshly and criticize than to pray, that's when you *really* have to dig in your heels and pray with the purpose of self-deliverance. No matter what you are asking God for, it is important that you faint not even when change is not immediate. Chances are, someone is still waiting to see the polished results of their prayers in your spiritual image as well. Praying for others is a ministry of service; it couples intercession with that of servant-hood. Notice how the scripture says that praying for others will also result in *your* healing.

> *Therefore confess your sins to each other and*
> *pray for each other so that you may be healed.*
> *The prayer of a righteous man is powerful and*
> *effective. James 5:16 NIV*

Through prayer, not criticism comes aid to both the person praying (indirect assistance) and the one needing prayer (direct assistance). Moving your prayer life into a ministry of service may be tough at first. However, it is a calling so linked to the authority and latitude of God's favor that we should all try to achieve it.

Anyone called to intercessory is endowed by God to function with this gift as an anointed vessel who is empowered by the name of Jesus. Since intercessory is not a job for wimps, one should also know that interceding on behalf of those you don't closely know or those who may even be your sworn enemy feels almost unnatural. But that's just it. When called to intercede, remember that the Spirit of the Lord within does not lead you by feelings. Even Hezekiah prayed for people who broke the rules of the Passover so that God might not smite them.

> *[He prayed,] 'May the Lord, who is good, pardon*
> *everyone who sets his heart on seeking God—the*
> *Lord, the God of his fathers- even if he is not*
> *clean according to the rules of the sanctuary.'*
> *And the Lord heard Hezekiah and healed the*
> *people.*
> *2 Chronicles 30:18b-20 NIV*

As a woman becomes a wife, her job is not only to cover her husband, but to also partner with him in accomplishing the goals that God has set before him. If this is difficult for a wife to conceptualize, imagine how much more difficult it is for a single woman who is called to intercede for a man she has yet to meet.

The work of becoming a wife begins the very moment God calls you to *wifedom*, the moment that He assures you that you will get married - one day. Early preparation is a battle that no one else can fight for you. It is prepared by the Lord for you to spiritually learn and actively discern strategic tactics like the ones you will most likely fight for your future husband and family in times of warfare. Of course nothing can really prepare you like the real thing, but Godly knowledge, wisdom, and discernment is also linked to a purpose-filled preparation. And looking at your role as a wife before you actually become one is nothing if not the application of Godly knowledge through early preparation.

Consequently, if you cannot, or more defiantly *will not*, fight to get your husband from the very beginning, who is to believe that you will have the will to really fight to keep him once he's yours? You may *think* that you will because of your strong desire to marry, but God knows whether or not you are really ready. Metaphorically, when you come to the point where you feel like you're going to pass out without your husband, that's exactly when the tests come. Sometimes, the Lord shows you better than He can tell you.

When you won't even rise early in the morning or in the middle of the night to pray for the husband and family that you believe you are ready for, know that it's in those moments that God uses the opportunity to show you that you're just not really ready for the husband He has for *you*. And no, not every woman that you meet has to go through this in order to get her husband. But wasn't that you who asked God to "bless me and enlarge my territory!" (1 Chronicles 4a:10 NIV)? Hopefully, you are aspiring for your marriage and partnership to be something quite different from what you have ever witnessed among others.

I can remember praying and asking the Lord to tailor me for the needs of my future husband, (receiving a tailor-made husband is not a bad thing, either). Let me clarify. Tailor-made does not mean passivity, robotic, or stifled. When God tailors two people in the partnership and commitment of marriage, it is a major part of the cleaving process beginning with the very foundation of the union's inception. Difficulty presents itself when you look at the unions of others and wonder, "Why not me, Lord?" Be careful! Proverbs 14:30 (NIV) cautions, "A heart at peace gives life to the body, but envy rots the bones." The point is this, looking at the relationships of others can only give you a very basic idea of what He has in store for you – perhaps it's the same story but alternate chapters in the same book.

Sometimes the outcome of your fight or struggle with timing and walking into victory will stem from your lack of self-confidence, because it's usually so different from what you've ever seen before. When you are on the outside looking in, you actually get a false-positive image of someone else's reality. In numerous cases, it is impossible to try to witness or recall another's calling that quite resembles the one to which you've been charged. But be careful once again! Looking with the wrong eye can be just as dangerous as listening to the wrong voices. According to Jesus, we each have our own unique path. Jesus' answer to Peter when he questioned another disciple's mission was,

> *If I will that he tarry till I come, what is that to*
> *thee? Follow thou me.*
> *John 21:22 KJV*

Beyond the message of minding one's business, the scripture emphasizes to walk in the dimension of the spirit and see things clearly with your spiritual eye. And the same is true with the spiritual ear. Discerning God's voice is imperative while walking through this journey and interceding for your husband-to-be.

Do you remember when you were in school and the nurse or physician performed hearing tests on you annually? Well, the Master Physician does that also, except much more frequently. I can remember a period of time where I would hear God talking to me distinctly and loudly in the middle of the night. There was one time when His voice was so loud that I actually thought someone was there in the house with me! But in actuality, those were my spiritual ears' hearing tests. I believe God was making sure that I knew His voice. More importantly, He wanted me to trust my own judgment of whose voice I was hearing so there would be no confusion or doubt in what He says. Saul is an example of a person who the Lord instructed, but who decided not to hear His voice and acted on decisions that were of his own volition. Samuel had to deliver the Lord's decision to reject Saul because he would no longer hear Him. Samuel asked,

> *'Does the Lord delight in burnt offerings and*
> *sacrifices as much as in obeying the voice of*
> *the Lord? To obey is better than sacrifice,*
> *and to heed is better than the fat of the rams.*
> *For rebellion is like the sin of divination, and*
> *arrogance like the evil of idolatry. Because*
> *you have rejected the word of the Lord, he has*
> *rejected you as king.'*
> *1 Samuel 15:22-23 NIV*

When God gave you the charge of interceding for the men in your life, great care and consideration went into that decision. Like Saul, don't put yourself in the predicament where your disobedience grieves the Lord because you have neglected your duties of servant-hood toward the men in God's army. Intercessory is about standing in the gap for those who cannot do it for themselves or who simply do not know what it is they need. Time with God is of the utmost importance because it is the only way revelation will come to you from the Holy Spirit. Prayer, fasting, and reading the Word all provide revelation to you.

Are you bold enough to make a difference in the life of the man you are asking God for? Are you bold enough to pray for the husband God hasn't even revealed to you yet? If God has called you to pray for someone, a friend, family member, or even a troublesome co-worker, that falls under the category of expected interceding. But what happens when He asks you to intercede for the really difficult ones – enemies, the seemingly already highly favored, or even the loathsome ex-boyfriend? That's not quite as easy to handle. Momentarily meditate and focus on this power principle. Even though God could use someone else, He chose you so that you would gain an opportunity to simultaneously receive and become a blessing.

When God uses you to intercede for another, understand that this is His way of doing a much-needed work in you as well. If you turn away opportunities to bless someone – your anointed job – you just might lose out on an opportunity of a lifetime, a chance to actually *be* a blessing. How can you say that you love God Whom you cannot see, when you do not honor His commands on love toward the person in need – whom you can see?

> *For anyone who does not love his brother, whom*
> *he has seen, cannot love God, whom he has*
> *not seen. And he has given us this command:*
> *Whoever loves God must also love his brother.*
> *1 John 4:20b-21 NIV*

Can you see the duplicity of becoming tired of praying for a man who needs your intercessory prayers now, yet pleading to God asking that He reveal your husband to you? And what about promising that you will actually pray for that future husband later as a wifely duty?

Selfishness of focus in helping one specific person often blinds us from helping those who truly need our prayers. Right now, for many of us, our husband's needs mirror those of the men who are already in our lives, those who need so much help, structure, prayer, leadership, and guidance. Prayer is God's cue, the necessary key to move and act in someone's life. Turning your back on these men could be comparable to turning your back on the one you so desperately want to help.

This charge that has been placed in your heart and in your spirit is really not about you. You may be the vehicle, the vessel that has been chosen by God, but don't think of the move of God as something solely for your benefit. He will get the glory through your testimony, and the person who is in need of the intercessory prayer is able to move mountains because of your ministry. If you are afraid, that really is alright. Joyce Meyer has a saying, "Do it afraid." In the end, you will reap the benefits of God's glory and also become the inspiration that someone else needs in order to make it through.

> *For God, who said, 'Let light shine out of*
> *darkness,' made his light shine in our hearts*
> *to give us the light of the knowledge of the*
> *glory of God in the face of Christ. But we*
> *have this treasure in jars of clay to show that*
> *this all-surpassing power is from God and not*
> *from us. We are hard pressed on every side,*
> *but not crushed; perplexed but not in despair;*
> *persecuted, but not abandoned; struck down, but*
> *not destroyed. We always carry around in our*
> *body the death of Jesus, so that the life of Jesus*
> *may also be revealed in our body.*
> *2 Corinthians 4:6-10 NIV*

What a blessing and a sense of fulfillment that overtakes you when you pray for protection, Godly knowledge, wisdom, and discernment for a person's life. Your intercessory prayer gives you the power to stop the devil's attack on those you care about and even those you've grown to love through this process. When you fast and pray, the Holy Spirit will actually give you the words. At some point, your prayers can ultimately be God's words out of your mouth, and like a melodious song, it becomes music right back to God's ears. You already know that His word cannot return to him void. Isaiah 55:11 (NIV) declares, "so is my word that goes out from my mouth: It will not return to me empty, but will accomplish what I desire and achieve the purpose for which I sent it."

God will reveal to you exactly what your prayer ought to be. This is yet another reason why a covenant relationship with the Lord is crucial. Quite a few years ago, I took an intercessory prayer class. Evangelist Selena Harris of New Destiny Fellowship church taught, "The motivation to intercede for others comes out of your love for the Lord." In that class, she instructed us that others around you will receive the overflow, the benefits of God's awesome power reflected through your relationship with Him.

Sometimes you may think that what you've been led to do is something that you have concocted in your own head or heart – something you told yourself to do instead of what God may have told you. Pondering these thoughts in your head tends to happen when you just can't quite figure out the purpose for it or the lesson in it. Sometimes when you play it out in your mind, you may feel like you cannot even share what God has told you, because in all probability, no one would understand. Who would believe you? You may even feel like you want to give up and throw in the towel. And when you realize that one of your best male friends is the man you are interceding for and someone else will end up with him and not you – that's when you want to pack it all in and claim there is no way that intercessory prayer works. Remember, "And those he predestined, he also called; those he called, he also justified; those he justified, he also glorified" (Romans 8:30 NIV).

That scripture is deeper than most people perceive. *Chosen* doesn't always mean the person was waiting in line for the challenge. Chosen can also mean God sees and uses the greater potential in us for the common good of those who love Him, even for the benefit of others. Realize today that our pain is not our own. You've heard the saying, *favor ain't fair*. Well, neither is the calling – especially the difficult ones. I'd like to extend those words by saying, *favor ain't fair and the calling ain't always calming*, at least not for all of us.

> "What He [God] has set up for your life no one else can handle or afford."
>
> (Youth Pastor Michelle Butler)

Chapter 10

If It's Early, It Could Die

$\mathcal{R}$evelation is truly an awesome gift from God! And since most of us are kids at heart, whether it is silently or out loud, we usually ask the question, "Why?" The funny thing is, most adults hate it when inquisitive children repeatedly ask *why*. Since we are more than likely the symbols of authority in conversations with them, it is rarely that we appreciate being questioned by those who are ill equipped to figure it out for themselves. I really believe God feels the same way about us questioning His authority, His timing, or His will. Nevertheless, even though I know this, sometimes I *still* can't help but to ask Him *why* or even how certain situations are going to turn out.

I can remember the periods of anxiety where I felt that I needed God to answer specific questions I had in order to pacify my doubts. I wanted God to tell me who my husband was, just how long I had to wait for him, and why he was taking so long to come and claim me as his wife. I remember one particular instance when for weeks, I couldn't even think straight; the questions kept mounting up, and I actually became irritable and hard to get along with. It was an awful feeling, and my attitude left much to be desired. Every aspect of the real me was completely out of character simply because I felt that

I had lost control of a situation I never had control over in the first place. I got so sick of my own self that I finally realized that I needed to pray for peace and forgiveness. I got quiet and remained still long enough to rest peacefully as I sought God – not His answers. Without warning, hesitation, or confusion, I heard from the Lord. On a long drive back from prayer, I felt these words utter in my spirit, "If it's early, it could die." Because I have an analytical mind, one word in particular stuck out to me; the word *could*. It was the possibility of death that intrigued me.

Think of this comparison in the natural. When a mother is pregnant, there comes a critical point when she can both see and feel the manifestation of God's promise in her life. Now although others can *see* the promise of God in her life as well, she's the one who can *feel* the fluttering and the stretching of the promise making room for its own growth. Because she watches it so very closely, she can often become anxious while waiting for the final moments of the promise's arrival. But although she may say, *I can't wait until this is over*, (the impatience) or *I wish this baby (the promise) would come now*, she really doesn't know the possible harm in what she is saying, because if she really could have the promise come too early, she might be terribly disappointed.

It is understood that there may be points during that process of change when that mother-to-be may feel the strongest urgency in really wanting that promise to come early. How does your situation fit this scenario? Understand that within that same process there is also a period of time when birthing the seed of promise before God's perfect timing *will* definitely result in death. Then there also comes a time, perhaps in the last stretch towards the end, when birthing that promise *could* result in death. Although the term *could* refer to a mere possibility, it may also prove just as deadly as if it were a *definite* result. The same is true for your seed – the promise of God to bring your husband to you. The right man at the wrong time could cause you to miss or barely recognize your blessing. The popular phrase '*Let go, and let God*' means totally casting your care on Him. He has not forgotten how long you've been waiting or how old you are, and He's even counted all of your tears. So cast your care, rest peacefully, wait patiently, and process easily.

Wifedom is not a destination; it's a journey – a process grouped by phases. Do you really believe it's God's intention for you to feel frustrated in your wait time? From experience, I know that is the furthest from the truth. You don't have to be a mother to appreciate the analogy of waiting out the full term of your *pregnancy* (seed bearing) to finally meet your *child* (the promise). As tired as one might feel in the last trimester, most women realize just how important it is for the child to stay in the womb, grow stronger and develop fully. The development and vitality of God's promise to you is no different. If birthed too soon, it *could* die.

From Bitter Pain Comes the Birthing of Instruction

Do you ever deal with the pressure of answering meaningless questions like, "Why aren't you married yet?" or my favorite one, "What are you waiting for before you get married and have kids?" Even some Christians ask these questions as if they don't know it's really out of your control. Don't they understand that technically you could go out there and marry the first man that asks you and have a baby? Handling the question itself can really be more difficult.

Although most people mean well and most likely don't want you to bear the weight of emotional anguish with such ridiculous questioning, often times it still leaves a small knot in your throat as you grapple for the words, "I'm waiting on the Lord," or "It's just not my time yet."

For a moment, don't you just wish everyone knew and accepted the truth as you have grown to do? Why has your singleness become a mission of solving Pandora's box for everyone else? How better off you would be if everyone realized that the Lord your God is the only One who can successfully orchestrate the meeting of your future Boaz and ignite the flames of your loving marriage. Let it be known, the barrenness of your promise is only a temporary pang but a noteworthy sacrifice of praise unto the Lord. Perhaps there are many women you know personally who can share in your stories of the secret, yet mental taunting and the silent double-minded feelings of questioning God's promise. But there is definitely one woman in the Bible who unquestionably would understand your anguish and frustration – and that woman is Hannah.

Refer to Hannah's situation as a self-mirrored image for the acts of obedience, submission to God's direction, and the ability to discern God's will – not as a private problem of anxiety, filled with ridicule and bouts of desperation. We all know that sometimes we can be our own worst enemy by allowing the real Enemy to use others against us or feed us false doctrine, which causes us to entertain thoughts of doubt and fear. But Hannah didn't do that. This is just why I look up to her. Hannah's actions are symbolic of what most *women in waiting* need to do. The Word instructs us to seek God's face.

> *Glory in his holy name; let the hearts of those*
> *who seek the Lord rejoice. Look to the Lord and*

his strength; seek his face always.
Psalm 105:3-4 NIV

When trouble faced Hannah, she took a bold step of faith and refused to face it. When the pains of her barrenness and feelings of emptiness came over her, she overcame them by facing God instead and seeking Him through prayer and deliverance.

> *Once when they had finished eating and drinking*
> *in Shiloh, Hannah stood up. Now Eli the priest*
> *was sitting on a chair by the doorpost of the*
> *Lord's temple. In bitterness of soul Hannah wept*
> *much and prayed to the Lord. And she made a*
> *vow, saying, 'O Lord Almighty, if you will only*
> *look upon your servant's misery and remember*
> *me, and not forget your servant but give her a*
> *son, then I will give him to the Lord for all the*
> *days of his life, and no razor will ever be used on*
> *his head.'*
> *1 Samuel 1:9-11 NIV*

Despite how she might have felt, I can picture Hannah throwing up her hands, about-facing against the winds of trouble, and heading off to the temple to seek the face of God. I believe Hannah's womb was purposely closed because just like so many of us, she had to get to the point where she was willing to do whatever was necessary for her to give herself over to the Lord – and seek God's presence, not His presents. Like Hannah, we have to guard our hearts against misplacing God's promise before Him. An enlightening statement in 2 Chronicles 26:5b (NIV) exhorts, "As long as he sought the Lord, God gave him success." How frustrated do you have to get in order to align your will up to God's will? Instead of facing your barren situation, seek God's face, not out of what you want Him to do, but out of His love for you.

The scriptures say "year after year" Elkanah left his town to worship and sacrifice unto the Lord (1 Samuel 1:3-5 NIV). Year after year Hannah went with him and was given something to sacrifice indicating that she had never truly made a sacrifice of her very own. All I can say is thank God for His patience. Hannah soon realized that *she* needed to make a promise to God, not God unto her. It was Hannah's vow to God that activated her faith. Then a sacrifice on her own from *her* heart was what the Lord needed to fulfill the promise. Although God did not cause her pain, Hannah's feelings of desperation were His call of action to her. She needed to voice the promise from within her own spirit.

Many of you are waiting for God to make you a promise when all along He has been waiting for you to decree a vow unto Him. After all you've been through with Him, by now you should know Him well enough to make a move, for He is with you. He's waiting for you to initiate the covenant because He has already made a promise to you the moment you gave your life over to Him. Are you confused about what that move ought to be? That's easy – what have you been asking Him for? How will you give it back to the Lord? How will you prepare it and give it back to Him to use at *His* will? Be honest with yourself. Are you truly prepared to give that marriage completely over to God as He instructs you? Would you willingly sacrifice some of your husband's time with you, his gifts, his touch, or his initial talents (worth)? How about the security of fully knowing about his physical health? Have you ever given thought to that before?

Magazines, television shows, and movies tend to make marriage look passion-filled and honeymoon-like most of the time, but the reality is far from their portion of the truth. What if God told you that your husband would lack the ability to hold you or fully satisfy you sexually? Would you still pledge that vow? Or what if He told you that you would enjoy the company of your husband for a short time like Hannah did her son before being carried off to be with the Lord in service? How easy is it to make a vow when you know that your circumstance will not look like others? Some of you will have to fight back the tears of happiness over finally receiving your Boaz while swallowing the lump in your throat, because neither he nor your marriage fits the mold you've dreamed about for so long. Can you still do it? Are you still willing to be the helpmate of the Boaz that God has in store for you – no matter what? These and others are tough questions one should ask before making the vow to God and the commitment to become one with the imperfections of another human being.

Chapter 11

Have a Deep Resolve – Firm Determination

*J*ust look how far you've come. God has given you a word; He's ordering your steps – making your crooked places straight, and has possibly or even recently announced a long sought-after promise over your life. You should feel like you're on top of the world at this point – but maybe, just maybe some of you still feel like something is missing or even empty. Perhaps it is that you still need to develop an attitude like God's attitude. Maybe you need to develop a deep resolve – the firm determination to enjoy the peace and restoration of God that comes when you get into complete agreement with whatever He is or isn't doing at this moment.

The Bible is full of stories of those who either tried to alter God's plan, failed in their faith through disobedience, or even ignored His instruction while stepping out of His perfect will and timing. And metaphorically speaking, Jonah is a prime example of all three. The story of Jonah is more than the *fish story* people usually connect it to in Sunday school. The book of Jonah is a reminder of what happens when we respond to God's instructions with blatant hesitation or disregard of His commands by purposefully heading in the opposite direction of His will. Let's take Jonah's dilemma for example. He was instructed to minister to his enemies on God's behalf and show love to the people he hated most. Now as hard as that may have been, the Bible does not say whether or not he initially tried to plead with God for a different task as some of us might have done. Instead, Jonah's initial actions simply expressed: *No, I'm not going to do it Lord.*

> *The word of the Lord came to Jonah son of*
> *Amittai: 'Go to the great city of Nineveh and*
> *preach against it, because its wickedness has come*
> *up before me.' But Jonah ran away from the*
> *Lord and headed for Tarshish. He went down to*
> *Joppa, where he found a ship bound for that*
> *port. After paying the fare, he went aboard and*
> *sailed for Tarshish to flee from the Lord.*
> *Jonah 1:1-3 NIV*

Jonah's hate for the Ninevites was very strong; one can only infer how deep that hatred must have been for him to refuse God's command to go to Nineveh. Although many historians believe the primary reason for his disobedience was due to his extreme loathing for the Ninevites, there might have indeed been another clear-cut yet overlooked explanation. Perhaps, just maybe Jonah was simply afraid of the outcome. If the Ninevites were saved, how would that have changed things for Jonah and the Israelites? How many times has God given you very distinct and explicit instructions to do something and instead of following through, you doubled back and doubted your ability to complete the task? Consequently, many who have found themselves in this situation mistakenly claim that they really didn't hear from God and continue to run in the completely opposite direction of their obligation.

Have you had a Jonah moment in your life yet? Jonah was instructed by the Lord to preach against what was going on in the city of Nineveh because its wickedness was against God. In adhering to God's command, Jonah's presence was necessary in that city. His job was deeper than just '*knee-mailing*' or praying in the spirit from afar. God directly and distinctly requested Jonah's presence to be seen, his voice to be heard, and his authority to radiate with God's aura from within. Do you see where I'm going with this? In order for you to have markers of success through your process, you need to first understand that everything that God instructs you to do is not going to be easy to understand or applicable without His direction.

The focus on Jonah is really a mirror for self. When was the last time you heard from the Lord – but instead of running toward His command, you tensed up, were overcome by fear, and nearly debated whether or not to deal with the consequences of your own disobedience? If you can claim just a mere part of this excuse, then Jonah's story may not be as far off from yours as one might think. Fear and lack of faith coupled together do ultimately lead to disobedience. And just like Jonah – the road to recovery and repentance is often a mountainous lesson designed by the Master Teacher Himself.

Jonah's probable feelings may have stemmed from his over-zealous concern and judgment of the Ninevite people – what they were and were not doing, their unrelenting and fruitless behavior, and more importantly, God's concern for their repentance. As Jonah preached to them, God's power was to manifest from Jonah's mouth into the hearts of the unsaved while it cleansed Jonah as well. Jonah's ministry was two-fold. Before ministering to the Ninevites, the Lord needed to personally minister to Jonah himself, because he needed to understand that his fruitlessness would eventually manifest itself as his inability to love the seemingly unlovable. All of this stems from what Prophetess Juanita Bynum calls *"matters of the heart."* Instead of operating out of a renewed spirit and a clean heart, poor Jonah was more than likely struggling with what his mind – his intellect and experience – was telling him about the people he was told to face and minister to. When was the last time God had to pause His plans *with* you in order to *deal* with you?

Try as you might, there is no escaping God – no denying His plan for your life. You may end up taking a different, sometimes more difficult route, but the end result is always the same – God's plan and His way! Our decision really is easy – will it be His way or a much harder way? Now, although Jonah took the more difficult route, he still managed not to lose any sleep at the bottom of that ship because he knew that eventually he would end up doing what God had commanded in the very beginning. It's no different than a child stalling from telling a parent right away that a detention must be served. The child figures the parent may find out sooner or later, and in that young person's mind, since a punishment is inevitable – it may as well be later rather than sooner.

> *Then the Lord sent a great wind on the sea,*
> *and such a violent storm arose that the ship*
> *threatened to break up. All the sailors were*
> *afraid and each cried out to his own god. And*
> *they threw the cargo into the sea to lighten the*
> *ship. But Jonah had gone below deck, where he*
> *lay down and fell into a deep sleep. The captain*
> *went to him and said, 'How can you sleep? Get*
> *up and call on your god! Maybe he will take*

notice of us, and we will not perish.'
Jonah 1:4-6 NIV

Jonah was not afraid at that point for his decision to run was already in affect. So why was he stalling for time? Ask the question of yourself. Why do any of us stall from the inevitable? Why run away from God's hand? How come so many of us toy with the possibility of His wrath and encircle the same mountain repeatedly? Even Jonah knew when it was time to face God and quit running away.

The sea was getting rougher and rougher. So
they asked him, 'What should we do to you to
make the sea calm down for us?' 'Pick me up
and throw me into the sea,' he replied, 'and it will
become calm. I know that it is my fault that this
great storm has come upon you.'
Jonah 1:11-12 NIV

Even though Jonah ran away from his initial responsibility, God still ended up using him in his state of delay through his disobedience. Oh yes, God will use all things; He's the only one that can make a message out of the mess we've made. In the end, when those men finally threw Jonah overboard, they gave themselves over to the Lord. Remember that God is always going to get the glory out of your test no matter how long it takes you, because in the end, all

Tests are not about punishment – they are about elevation through revelation.

(Latoyia K. Bailey, PhD)

He ever really wants to do is bring you up higher in Him anyway.

That's what it's all about. Tests are not about punishment – they are about elevation through revelation. Right now you are most likely the closest you have ever been to your next level – the dawning of those dreams God put on the inside of you is on the horizon of the mess you're dealing with right now. So you might as well know that a big part of overcoming obstacles in your path is similar to a triathlon. Crossing the finish line means taking a deeper breath than usual and pushing pass your personal pains, while simultaneously encouraging others that are coming from behind you to make it pass their own personal leaps and bounds as well.

Feeling responsible for the men's trouble, Jonah instructed them to throw him overboard so that the great storm and the raging sea would become calm again. The Lord could have let Jonah die right there in the middle of the ocean – alone, afraid, and even in sin for he had not yet repented for his disobedience. Instead, Jonah's testimony was taking form because the Lord still gave him provision and even shelter in the midst of his mess for " . . . the Lord provided a great fish to swallow Jonah, and Jonah was inside the fish three days and three nights" (Jonah 1:17 NIV).

For three days Jonah remained in the belly of that fish – God's own consecrated *think tank* set apart for Jonah's very personal death, burial, and resurrection. Why a fish? Of all the creatures of the sea, why did the Lord send the ever-watchful fish? Although forthcoming, the fish became a sign among those who shared the Christian faith during the biblical days of persecution. In the case of Jonah's dilemma, the once-secret symbol of the fish became the Lord's metaphoric holding pen for Jonah to *die to self* and realize that he held the keys of authority throughout his own period of persecution. Needless to say, his affliction could have lasted much longer than three days. Isn't it amazing that God knows exactly what methods to use to get our undivided attention? Jehovah Tsidkenu is the only one that knows exactly how much pressure to apply for us to comply without breaking us in two during the process of transforming us into someone who is more selfless than self-centered. Jonah needed a very unique kind of pressure.

From inside the fish Jonah prayed to the Lord
his God. He said: 'In my distress I called to the
Lord, and he answered me. From the depths of
the grave I called for help, and you listened to my
cry. You hurled me into the deep, into the very
heart of the seas, and the currents swirled about
me; all your waves and breakers swept over me.
I said, 'I have been banished from your sight;
yet I will look again toward your holy temple.'
The engulfing waters threatened me, the deep
surrounded me; seaweed was wrapped around my
head. To the roots of the mountain I sank down;
the earth beneath barred me in forever. But you
brought my life up from the pit, O Lord my God.'
Jonah 2:1-6 NIV

Death, burial, and resurrection is not about a physical death – it's about a fleshly death. To the men on that boat, it must have looked like Jonah's life had come to an abrupt end. To anyone on the outside looking in, it must have seemed as though his physical life was over. But God had other intentions. Jonah's death was about a separation – his separation from sin, carnal behaviors, and unrighteous attitudes.

In order for the Lord to deal with him, he had to be set apart from all others so that God could deal with him alone. The Lord had to become his Jehovah Shammah – the ever-Present One and the only One on whom he would totally depend. How could God continue to use Jonah in his present state? How could God catapult him to the next level when he was too self-centered to see God's hand over his own life or over the situation with the Ninevites? Some things had to die in him. And with the mirror of truth in front of you, ask yourself what must die in you. What are the very attitudes, fears, or mannerisms that must die in you? Or perhaps you are like Jonah; you won't even know that these attitudes exist until the Lord sends *your* big fish – your holding pen.

The Triad Experience

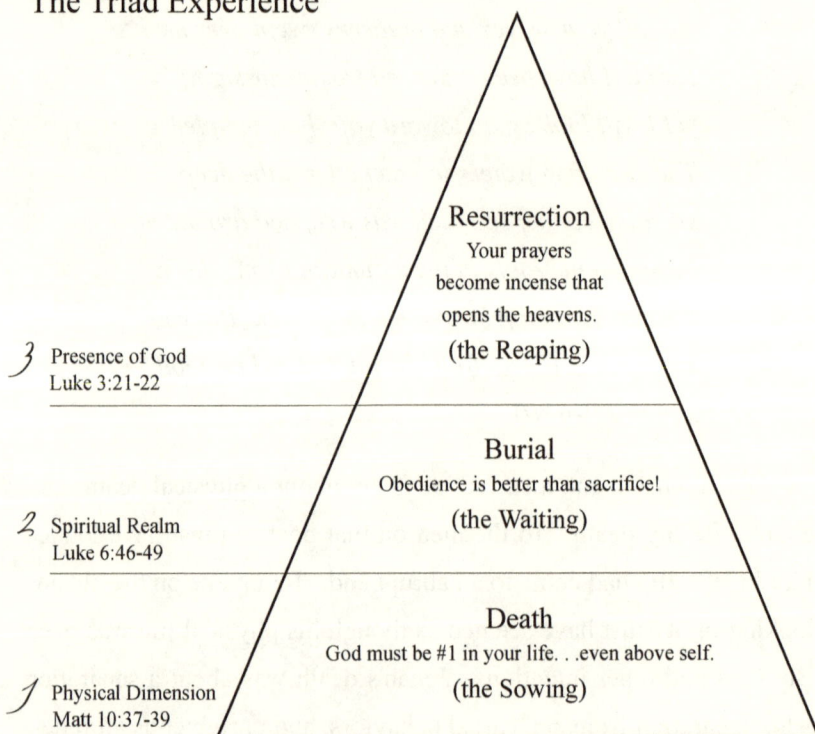

Resurrection
Your prayers become incense that opens the heavens.
(the Reaping)

3 Presence of God
Luke 3:21-22

Burial
Obedience is better than sacrifice!
(the Waiting)

2 Spiritual Realm
Luke 6:46-49

Death
God must be #1 in your life. . .even above self.
(the Sowing)

1 Physical Dimension
Matt 10:37-39

The "Triad Experience" is a pyramid, which serves as a visual depiction illustrating the process God used to take Jonah through a crossover from being led by the selfishness of his carnality to the fearlessness of his repentance. And notice that his prayer did not curse the hand of God that formed his test. The fish was never sent to kill him but rather to protect him through his death, burial, and resurrection experience. It really does not pay to curse the burden, which provides the bridge that leads you into the presence of God. Jonah could have allowed his fears and his emotions to dictate the fight that was necessary for him to survive through the test. In the darkest part of that test, in the belly of that fish, life was probably at its bleakest. But like Jonah, it is imperative that you fight even when you do have a promise from the Lord. It's often easy for people to give up or throw in the towel when they know that God has something big in store for them. It's just easier to step aside, let God do it and step back in when He has finished the work. That's a lie from the enemy. When God decrees a thing, it will happen. But you are the one that can kill the seed. The warrior in you has to live in order for the seed to grow. You often have to fight even harder for it because if you give up, someone else can come along and reap the benefits of what God intended for you to sow.

Ministering to the Ninevites was indeed part of Jonah's testimony. What is the current test that will ultimately shape your future testimony? Understand that it is something that you must go through *alone*. Your big fish was never designed to take anything from you. The Lord is only

"Life's not about running from storms, but learning how to dance in the rain. God is love."

(Rev. Run)

trying to get something *through* you so He can get something *to* you.

> *This service that you perform is not only supplying*
> *the needs of God's people but is also overflowing*
> *in many expressions of thanks to God. Because of*
> *the service by which you have proved yourselves,*
> *men will praise God for the obedience that*
> *accompanies your confession of the gospel of*
> *Christ, and for your generosity in sharing with*
> *them and with everyone else. And in their prayers*
> *for you their hearts will go out to you, because of*
> *the surpassing grace God has given you. Thanks*
> *be to God for his indescribable gift!*
> *2 Corinthians 9:12-15 NIV*

This is no mathematical equation, but it is an important part of the *laws of ministry*. It's about reaching toward the level of completion. After your resurrection experience, you will then have the keys of authority to help others get through their own triad experience. This may or may not come as a surprise, but the resurrection is not really about you. Get your mind off yourself for once. It is clearly about restoration, power, and authority. Your ministry will become greater and your relationship with God will certainly come up higher because the clutter will have all been removed when you enter into the Presence of the Lord.

Chapter 12

Be Happy, Be Free, and Be Filled!
Allow God to Get the Glory Out of Your Story

What are the things that make you happy – genuinely happy
with a face glowing of peace? Seriously think about it for a minute
because I'm not asking you what you *want* to make you happy. No.
I'm asking you what things are currently in your life that make you
happy and fill your heart with gladness. Be honest with yourself
because this question is very important. For example, I used to really
believe in my heart that being married and having children would
bring me unspeakable joy and happiness. And although it most likely
would bring me some level of contentment and fulfillment, truthfully
speaking, it may also come with unpredictable periods of questioning
or doubt. But as long as I believed there was unending bliss in marriage
and failed to consider the concept behind *the grass is greener on the
other side*, it was also probable that my fantasy could become quite
disappointing, if only a mere fraction of it became reality. So, again,
what makes you genuinely happy with a face glowing of peace?

Realizing that I was on this side of the grass and that I needed to
be happy here was truly a learning experience. I had to allow God

to teach me how to be happy. Can you believe that? I actually had an issue with finding peace and accepting true happiness as a single woman on a day-to-day basis. After quite some time, I realized that those things that bring total peace and a wealth of happiness into my life are already here. I really had to step back and count my many blessings, because daily I would often overlook them while I was busy believing the grass was greener on the other side of the fence.

In stepping back, I asked the Lord for help – help with becoming happy and at peace with my life. The words "look ahead" and "finish" kept ringing in my spirit. The funny thing was, whenever I would ask God for a word, I would keep hearing those same words in my spirit over and over again in one form or another. At first, I did not know what they meant. Believe me, trying to figure out if God's words were figurative or literal was yet another lesson in itself. I had to remember all that I had learned

> "Peace is being in a state of contentment with God no matter what's going on around you."
>
> (Yolanda Adams)

from past experiences – to just keep still in the natural as well as in the spiritual and God's words would become clear. *Look ahead* and *finish* were indeed the very words I needed to adhere to, because the future was already laid out and ordered by the Lord. They were already a manifestation of my everyday life. I was *already* operating in His plan, *but* I had to finish the work He had placed in me before moving onward to the next step. That's why I could not see anything.

Not only was I selfish in my own willful attempts, I was also preoccupied with my future (the promise). I was just a little unappreciative of the blessings God had already provided. My preoccupation and anxious feelings of the future were actually sinful. They woefully showed my lack of trust in God's plan and His timing. The Lord had called me to write and publish – the ministry of the pen became a viable tool that He would use to minister to many of His daughters who are also plagued by some of the very same questions that He had already revealed and answered for me.

The gift of writing had been with me for a long time, and I liked doing it. But for an even longer time, it had not been used to glorify God or His Kingdom, and it didn't always bring me joy. What good are our gifts if they are not a bridge between the edification of God's people and the actual manifestation of the blessings that are shut-up in the heavenly realm? Romans 11:29 (NIV) declares, *God's gifts and his call are irrevocable*. Our gifts and the calling on our lives are interchangeable and connected to one another.

I was searching for peace. It's as simple as that. I craved peace in my singleness and, in doing the work that the Lord had set out for me, I had finally found it. One of the most profound *principles of peace* is to look at those things that are unseen as though they really are seen – focus on the spiritual realm rather than the natural. We understand that this is only accomplished through faith, but so many also forget that faith must actually be activated in order for it to work. In short, faith leads to a promotion of peace.

In Proverbs 12:20 (NIV), it states, "there is deceit in the hearts of those who plot evil, but joy for those who promote peace." Therefore, having the joy of the Lord is an attitude that one must put on with a purpose. It has to be a conscious effort. Each day, you have to decide – make a selfless decision to be happy regardless of what you see, what you don't have, or how you feel carnally. This is spiritual warfare – there is a preparation before the storms of life come raging.

Every day, try to purpose in your spirit that you will put on happiness, just as you had to strive to put on righteousness and truth. And although realistically speaking, every single day won't be without its tests, as long as you have purposed happiness, you will equip yourself with all the necessary tools for combating sadness, bitterness, anger, depression, and more.

I think about Ruth and the *work* God set before her – the care and interdependence of her mother-in-law Naomi. Day in and day out she went into those fields to glean wheat in order to take care of not only herself but someone else as well. Her selfless acts were not those of a showy nature or of a means to an end. Ruth was happy in her work because it was indeed a part of her ministry duties unto God. And because she served happily, she was actually noticed by Boaz while serving - completing what she had started. "A happy heart makes the face cheerful, but heartache crushes the spirit" (Proverbs 15:13 NIV).

Ruth serves as an important example of peace, happiness, and contentment with her singleness. If one was to check her motives for taking such good care of Naomi or question her intentions for gleaning and working in those fields, it is probably less than likely that anyone would find as much as a blemish with her character and ability to love outside of her own needs. Even when Ruth realized that she had caught the attention of Boaz, she still kept focused on what her mission was – that of service to her beloved mother-in-law. Even though Boaz was in a position to care and provide for Ruth, she had never fully put all of her hope and expectation for provision in him. Her expectation was in the Lord.

> *So Ruth gleaned in the field until evening. Then she*
> *threshed the barley she had gathered, and it amounted*
> *to about an ephah. She carried it back to town, and*

her mother-in-law saw how much she had gathered.
Ruth 2:17-18 NIV

Like Ruth, the Lord will use you to be a light in someone else's dark times, but you cannot be a light for others if you are only concerned about yourself and your problems. So many people quote this scripture, "My help comes from the Lord, the Maker of heaven and earth" (Psalm 121:2 NIV) as a daily affirmation but never truly internalize it. Happily busy yourself in the ministry of helping others and God will work things out for you in your times of struggle as well. Ruth didn't even know that Boaz was making an easier way for her to complete her *work* – the task of serving which the Lord placed on her heart. How is the Lord making provisions for you, carving out a ministry for you to lead someone else toward healing as He leads you to finish *your* work?

> *Therefore we do not lose heart. Though outwardly*
> *we are wasting away, yet inwardly we are being*
> *renewed day by day. For our light and momentary*
> *troubles are achieving forgiveness and eternal glory*
> *that far outweighs them all. So we fix our eyes not*
> *on what is seen, but on what is unseen. For what is*
> *seen is temporary, but what is unseen is eternal.*
> *2 Corinthians 4:16-18 NIV*

Come out of the habit of letting your outward struggle be your inward muzzle – one that blankets the quietness in your spirit. Regardless of what is going on outside (the natural), allow your spirit to be renewed on the inside. Remember that everything has a set time, a *due season*. What task must you *do* before it's *due*? Continue to stand on God's promise as He delivers your future into your present.

Walking around unhappily with a frowned face and sour disposition is yet another example of an outward expression of one's lack of faith. Quite the opposite should be happening. Instead of magnifying your problems, magnify the Lord! Your faith during the tough times is made stronger when you think on the good things God has already done for you – how He already brought you through much tougher times and circumstances than you have had in the past.

The night before I was scheduled to defend my dissertation for my doctorate, everything that could have gone wrong actually did. My father became ill and was admitted into the hospital. Now my mother, being the ever-constant protector that she is, kept it from me for fear it would have made me too nervous to defend my work the next day. My father's becoming ill was indeed a set-up by the enemy so that I could fail. When that didn't work, the deceiver pulled out an even bigger gun. Hours before I would wake up and claim my victory of becoming the first PhD doctor in my family, I received a jaw-dropping call from a committee member. Apparently, there was almost a chapter's worth of work that needed revision and editing. You cannot even imagine the level of disbelief and horror that I was feeling at that moment. I almost hyperventilated as I took that call more seriously than I had taken anything else in my short-lived life.

As I started driving and maneuvering my way through rush hour traffic, I knew that I needed someone to speak words of encouragement to me. Believe me, I know there are many times when a woman must minister to herself, but that was not one of them. Let me tell you, after crying hysterically, partly out of fear but more out of sleep deprivation, my mother's ever-calming voice brought me back to reality. Her words were as clear as Paul's in the book of Romans. As sincere as any nurturing mother's voice could possibly be, mine reminded me that it was already done.

> *Yet he did not waver through unbelief regarding*
> *the promise of God, but was strengthened in his*
> *faith and gave glory to God, being fully persuaded*
> *that God had power to do what he had promised.*
> *Romans 4:20-21 NIV*

Paul's words echoing through my mother's love reminded me that faith comes when you exercise it. I had to exercise the muscle of faith by announcing to my spirit what I already knew about the Lord: "So then faith cometh by hearing, and hearing by the word of God" (Romans 10:17 KJV). When you couple the Word of God with the outward confessions of what He's already done for you, then you have indeed armed yourself with the boundless faith that is necessary to pull you out of the near endless emotional pit and into a sanctuary of peace that no one around you can quite understand. Remember, *tough times don't last but tough people do.*

Look to the Hills...

As close as I am to my mother, sister-friends, and other confidants, I have come to realize that all of my expectations and hopes of provision truly rest in the Lord – most certainly not in people. It's not that they won't love and support you at your darkest moments, but we have to understand that they are virtually incapable of filling that reserved void or empty space that can only be filled by the Lord. It is imperative that we accept this phenomenon because if we don't, then we hold our loved ones to a much higher standard than they are equipped to handle.

And, if you walk into your God-ordained partnership (marriage) with this attitude, you are already trying to place a weight on your husband that may only cripple him in the process and stifle your relationship before it even starts. Putting all of your hopes in another person is problematic because people have their own strongholds, fears, doubts, inhibitions, predispositions, and shortcomings. This is exactly why our hope ought to be in the Lord – not in people.

No matter how much the person loves you, unfortunately over time and through various experiences, you will be challenged to face a few let downs because the love of people can only go so far. Your overall peace and connection to God was bought with a blood covenant. And now, since Jesus has redeemed your life with His precious blood, looking to a mere person for the keys to your happiness is almost blasphemous and extremely hypocritical since you claim that you love and trust in Him. Instead of being too dependent upon man, remember to exercise your faith walk and repeat, "I lift up my eyes to the hills – where does my help come from? My help comes from the Lord, the Maker of heaven and earth" (Psalm 121:1-2 NIV).

As you look to the hills, at some point you will have to examine your level of intimacy with the Lord. Because we may have had very backwards and misshapen relationships with men in the past, we don't really understand that there are many facets to the word intimacy and the most important of these are not even sexual. In terms of intimacy with the Lord, this is your golden opportunity to freely open yourself up to Him, willingly uncover your nakedness, and personally invite Him into the deepest corners of your heart. There is no other level of intimacy closer than that! When this type of intimacy with the Lord exists, then "... do not grieve, for the joy of the Lord is your strength" (Nehemiah 8:10 NIV). Because the saying never gets old, I often meditate to *allow the Lord to get the glory out of your story.*

Every morning that you wake up, encourage yourself and say, "I will be happy on purpose." Here again is another opportunity to arm yourself for victory and fight the devil through spiritual warfare. It's not about walking around with a fake smile plastered on your face. Quite the contrary, being happy on purpose means you are not going to quit at what God has instructed you to do simply because it's gotten harder. The old saying is true – anything worth having is worth fighting for. Declaring to yourself that you won't quit and that you will not give up means fighting the good fight of faith.

You have to be a warrior. How can you tell God that you are willing to fight for your husband or any of God's promises when you won't even fight for your self - your peace, your sanity, your ultimate happiness? This type of fight is not about weaponry and ungodly tongue-lashings. It's about girding yourself with the armor of truth and confessing truth right out of your own mouth on a daily basis.

> *Do not be deceived: God cannot be mocked. A man reaps what he sows. The one who sows to please his sinful nature, from that nature will reap destruction; the one who sows to please the Spirit will reap eternal life. Let us not become weary in doing good, for at the proper time we will reap a harvest if we do not give up.*
> *Galatians 6:7-9 NIV*

Be anxious for nothing. Like Ruth, tend to the fields, the work that God has already laid before you. Remember – to busy yourself with a promise too soon (out of God's timing) is to labor in vain (operating in works of the flesh).

SEX B4 Marriage: The Real BFF
(Broken Future Fantasies)

If you are anything like me, this is usually the section of any singles' ministry book that you would skip to and read first. I finally stopped to ask myself why that had become my habit. As these books highlight what God's Word says about sex, most of the books on this issue say almost the same thing because God's Word has not changed. In this 21st Century, technologically savvy generation, many people have assumed that God's Word has indeed changed to catch up with the backwards standards of the world.

I have even watched and have heard many other Christians confess their belief that in this day and time, it's not likely that a man will wait for sex until marriage. And my answer to that is simply this: as long as we continue to make excuses for what we are not willing to wait for, then the men in our lives will not see the need to wait either because,the urgency and energy are placed in the wrong direction. We are not animals in the sense that we cannot control the urges or feelings that we have. The men and women of God have to exercise the muscle of self-control if we want to be blessed of the Lord and enjoy all of the fruits of marriage.

Often times, sex is misconstrued as the most important level of intimacy that exists within a relationship. However, this is a far cry from the truth. The truth is, countless relationships have ended bitterly after the flames of one's sexual desires either uncontrollably burned out or were smothered by premature thoughts of future commitments. Although the story of the relationship between brother and sister Amnon and Tamar is more about the issues of sex, manipulation, and control (through rape), its symbolism bears an uncanny resemblance to the many relationships that fail to survive under the crushing weight of those built solely on sexual conquests fueled by unbridled feelings and fleshly emotions.

> *Amnon became frustrated to the point of illness on account of his sister Tamar, for she was a virgin, and it seemed impossible for him to do anything to her. Now Amnon had a friend named Jonadab son of Shimeah, David's brother. Jonadab was a very shrewd man. He asked Amnon, 'Why do you the king's son, look so haggard morning after morning? Won't you tell me?' Amnon said to him, 'I'm in love with Tamar, my brother Absalom's sister.' 'Go to bed and pretend to be ill,' Jonadab said. 'When your father comes to see you, say to him, 'I would like my sister Tamar to come and give me something to eat. Let her prepare the food in my sight so I may watch her and then eat it from her hand.'*
> *2 Samuel 13:2-5 NIV*

Flesh *is* a powerful thing. However, it is only more powerful than the spirit if it is fed while the spirit is starved. Just like Amnon, if we chose to go around and think about sex or often dwell on unclean or non-beneficial thoughts about our inner *me*, then of course we make it a little more difficult to fight those fires of sexual desires that run through our minds. There are too many of us that have at least one friend like Jonadab who we often turn to when we want someone else to help fan the flames of our emotional embers – although we usually know they are wrong from the very beginning.

> *David sent word to Tamar at the palace: 'Go to the*
> *house of your brother Amnon and prepare some food*
> *for him.'. . . Then Amnon said to Tamar, 'Bring the*
> *food here into my bedroom so I may eat from your*
> *hand.' And Tamar took the bread she had prepared*
> *and brought it to her brother Amnon in his bedroom.*
> *But when she took it to him to eat, he grabbed her*
> *hand and said, 'Come to bed with me, my sister.'*
> *'Don't, my brother!' she said to him. 'Don't force*
> *me. Such a thing should not be done in Israel!*
> *Don't do this wicked thing. What about me? Where*
> *could I get rid of my disgrace? And what about*
> *you? You would be like one of the wicked fools in*
> *Israel. Please speak to the king; he will not keep me*
> *from being married to you.' But he refused to listen*
> *to her, and since he was stronger than she, he raped*
> *her. Then Amnon hated her with intense hatred.*
> *In fact, he hated her more than he had loved her.*
> *Amnon said to her, 'Get up and get out!'*
> *2 Samuel 13:7, 10-15 NIV*

Amnon's sexual act of selfishness, lust, and betrayal ended with Tamar's mental anguish and emotional death and his own natural death at the hands of their own brother Absalom. Some may wonder what Tamar's story has in common with today's version of sex before marriage existing in a relationship. Although that may be a fair question, its really not that hard to see. Look at how many lives were changed forever due to Amnon's decision: his act resulted in his death; his brother became a murderer; his sister's virginity and good name was stolen, and a father was forced to mourn for all of his children. Can you imagine the despair their father must have felt when he realized he was not there to save his own daughter from the awful trappings of his own son? Can you imagine how your Father would feel if you were overpowered by sex? This is just food for thought. Like David's children, every single person involved lost out on something vital that could not be won back. Of course forgiveness does continue to reign thanks to the love of Jesus, but God does not overlook habitual sin. Often times we delay or even destroy our own futures by placing sex on a higher pedestal than we ought!

STDs, broken hearts, and unplanned pregnancies are the usual outcomes so many of us are used to hearing. Even that isn't strong enough Kryptonite to scare the so-called toughest superwomen. But then there are those stories that leave us wondering *why did I* or *didn't I....* as we lay awake in the middle of the night. For example, I have openly heard women confess in their sister circles how they regretted the mistake of sleeping with someone they once considered marrying during the courtship. Yes, I know that part happens often. Measuring the performance of a husband prospect against a former love interest could cause one to see a healthy relationship like one sees an image in a fun-house mirror – distorted.

There are too many dangers in sitting around and comparing any part of the misgivings of the past to the newness of the future. The God-ordained man that comes into your life is not supposed to resemble "the other guy". That should be one of the bells or whistles that tell you to reevaluate the situation. Your husband is not supposed to be comparable with the men of your past. When God takes you to the next level of blessing in Him, it is not suppose to resemble the past. I'm sure that many of these women realized their error in judgment but did so too late. When this happens, sometimes women are forced to replay a what-could-have-been CD over and over in their minds. This was never God's intention. In the matter of sexual intimacy before marriage, God's promptings are not His outright denials. They are simply His safety nets – His method of getting something to us, not taking something away from us.

Sometimes talk shows and girlfriend gossip circles offer some of the best insight as to what people are thinking about sex – how they actually handle that level of intimacy or the commitment to abstain from it. There was one particular radio program where the host posed a question about saved women and oral sex. Yes! I went straight there – to a topic of sex many Christians would rather not openly discuss. As a matter of fact, that terminology was almost foreign in my grandparents' day. It seems that the discussion in our schools and in our churches of whether or not oral sex is actually considered sex is an obviously avoided question yet, the act itself is running rampant. This topic does not warrant a whole lot of discussion but it does need to be addressed. "....The body is not meant for sexual immorality, but for the Lord, and the Lord for the body" (1 Corinthians 6:13b NIV).

Sex using any member of your body is still considered sex. Let's not be fooled by the true meaning of abstinence or try to fool others with our blanketed versions of it. Believe as Paul believed, "Everything is permissible for me" – but not everything is beneficial. "Everything is permissible for me" – but I will not be mastered by anything (1 Corinthians 6:12 NIV). Paul is very clear in his practical advice to us about the issues of sex before marriage. Instead of considering his tone damning, think of it as an opportunistic, personal glimpse into what could be a very big mistake.

Stand Still + Calm Down = Watch God

For those of you that find it difficult, an excellent way to get your mind off the sex you are not having is to ask God for your personal GPS system – the direction for you to busy yourself with, as you are being a blessing to others. This may call for a newfound level of faith – one where you will have to stand still. Some people get a little confused by God's words *stand still*. It simply means for us to get out of God's way. We often do more harm than good when placing our hands in His business, those areas that are knowingly out of our reach and may actually prolong the process. Look at Sarah and Abraham. Instead of innately believing God's promise, Sarah laughed at it (Genesis 18:12 NIV). She put her hands in what was God's business and created quite a mess with Hagar. Her anxiety and inability to stand still caused strife within her own home and further delayed God's promise just because it did not make sense to her. Stop looking in your mind, which may be

> "The only way to feel victory is to learn how to do what's right even when it *feels* wrong."
>
> (Joyce Meyer)

blocked by limits, to make sense of God's monumental ways.

When you stand still, you are actually working on those things that God told you to fix, asked you to change, or prompted you to shed from your life. You are also placed in that position to help, minister, and usher others to the Lord by your walk, speech, attitude, song, smile, gifts, etc. This really is the time for the finishing touches before your Boaz shows up. Who knows, this might just be when he notices you – while you're working in the *fields*.

In whatever position God has you – friend, girlfriend, or wife – place your heart in His hands and trust that your positioning is a part of His set timing. Although there are times when it becomes more challenging than others, don't delay God's process by murmuring, grumbling, or complaining because the act of those behaviors is *not* against the actual situation alone, but against God Himself.

> *We should not test the Lord, as some of them did –*
> *and were killed by snakes. And do not grumble, as*
> *some of them did – and were killed by the destroying*
> *angel. These things happened to them as examples*
> *and were written down as warnings for us, on whom*
> *the fulfillment of the ages has come. So, if you think*
> *you are standing firm, be careful that you don't fall!*
> *1 Corinthians 10: 9-12 NIV*

When we are negative and constantly question the Lord with whys and how comes, we aren't really trusting Him. Ultimately what happens when we cannot find peace is that we become selfishly led into works of the flesh – that which is out of the will of God. When the Israelites went out of God's will with their grumbling, complaining, and fault finding, they remained on the backside of the desert for forty years because they showed themselves ill-prepared to walk into the promise land.

What are you showing God about your preparation toward your personal *promise land*? Now is the time for you to really be open and honest with yourself. Believe in the words Evangelist Jeremiah Cummings wrote in his book *Reaching For The World*, that "*When truth is on time it shall have no opposition.*" Do you really need to go back around your mountain and repeat your lessons, or are you now enlightened and further developed in your capability of handling the walk that God has been preparing for you – the walk into your promised land? Steady yourself through God's process using much prayer, patience, and poise; then proceed at God's pace with power and praise as you prepare yourself for your ultimate God-ordained wifedom position.

Steadying yourself and preparing yourself are self-help phrases as is the phrase '*encourage yourself*', but there are times you may feel ill-equipped to do so. As often as you need to – fortify yourself by praying this **Prayer of God's Anointed Appointed** and meditate daily on the Word of God. This will help you as you stand on the promise He has already made you and help you to climb the ladder of your high calling.

Lord, allow Your Word, through the sound of my voice, to be an effectual and fervent prayer breaking the yoke of instability and faithlessness. Today I come boldly before Your throne of grace to command those things you have allowed me to see in the heavenly realm to manifest in the earthly one. Continue to show me the power in this partnership – the continuity when Your Spirit flows within me. Father, reveal to me the needs, pains, fears, and strongholds of my husband so that I may intercede as you have ordained. Help me to realize the distractions set before me by the enemy that would cause me to miss my appointed time with destiny. Help me to understand my purpose and to commit myself to the ministry of sowing into the future of my covenant relationship. Help me to be more effected by what I know in the spirit rather than

what I see in the natural. Increase my perseverance
to finish Your work in me so that I may be mature and
complete, not lacking anything *(James 1:4 NIV). For*
the purpose of growth in You and maturing into wifedom,
Lord teach me that my feelings don't get to vote. Never
let me forget that the ruler of the world cannot measure
Your Word over my life. Help me to have my spiritual
eyes wide open and the discipline in the spirit to pray
without ceasing. Lord, I want to walk boldly in my
present season. I want to be content in the purpose of
growth in my singleness. Lord, I want to be stretched and
grow onward and move forward into the ministry of my
calling. Lord, I want more of You – more of You to fill
more of me. I need to partnership with You in the spirit
so that I may be a blessing in the lives of others. Now
Father, as You help me to stand on my promise, help me to
climb that ladder toward a higher calling.

In Jesus' name,

Amen